The Double Eagle Guide to

WESTERN
STATE
PARKS

VOLUME 4
DESERT SOUTHWEST

ARIZONA
NEW MEXICO
UTAH

A DOUBLE EAGLE GUIDE™

DISCOVERY PUBLISHING
BILLINGS, MONTANA USA

The Double Eagle Guide to Western State Parks
Volume 4   Desert Southwest

Fourth Edition

Published by:

Discovery Publishing
Post Office Box 50545
Billings, Montana 59105 USA

Discovery Publishing is an independent, private enterprise. The information contained
herein should not be construed as reflecting the publisher's approval of the policies
or practices of the public agencies listed.

Information in this book is subject to change without notice.

Front Cover, all volumes: A Pacific Northwest state park
selected to represent all of the West's great state parks.

Frontispiece, Volume 4: Cimarron Canyon State Park, New Mexico

10 9 8 7 6 5 4 3 2 1

June 20, 2007   9:03 AM Mountain Time

Produced, printed, and bound in the United States of America.

ISBN 978-1-932417-18-0

▤ TABLE OF CONTENTS

Double Eagle™ Guides

❦ INTRODUCTION TO THE *Double Eagle*™ SERIES ❦

State parks are relative newcomers to the overall public lands picture. While the establishment of Earth's national parks dates back to 1872 with the creation of Yellowstone National Park, state parks have come to the fore of scenic, recreational and historic importance mainly in the latter half of the Twentieth Century. Although history is uncertain as to just when and where the first state park was established, what *is* certain is the overwhelming acceptance and support given to the state park concept by the citizens and visitors of the United States.

Whether you're a veteran of many Western trips or are planning your first visit, this series is for you.

In the *Double Eagle*™ series, our goal is to provide you with reliable, comprehensive, and yet concise, *first-hand* information about these parks—special places which tend to offer more simple (perhaps even more 'natural') enjoyment than that which can be experienced among the awesome spectacles of the West's national parks.

The volumes which comprise the *Double Eagle*™ series constitute a significant departure from the sketchy, plain vanilla approach to information provided by other guidebooks. Here, for the first time, is the most *useful* information about the West's most *useable* public parks. We've included a broad assortment of state parks from which you can choose: From simple, free parks, to areas in deluxe, landscaped surroundings.

The name for this critically acclaimed series was suggested by the celebrated United States twenty-dollar gold piece—most often called the *"Double Eagle"*—the largest and finest denomination of coinage ever issued by the U.S. Mint. The *Double Eagle* has long been associated with the history of the West, as a symbol of traditional Western excellence.

So, too, the *Double Eagle*™ series seeks to provide you with information about the hundreds of small treasures owned, operated, and overseen (but, hopefully, never overlooked) by the citizens of the Western United States.

We hope you'll take pleasure in reading these pages, and come to use the information to enhance your own appreciation for the scenic, recreational and historic legacies of the Western United States.

We hope you'll enjoy your trip!

Thomas and *Elizabeth Preston*
Publishers

🛖 CONVENTIONS USED IN THIS SERIES Δ

The following conventions or standards are used throughout the *Double Eagle*™ series as a means of providing a sense of continuity between one park and the next.

Whenever possible, the parks within each state have been arranged in what we have determined to be a reasonable progression, and based on *typical travel patterns* within a region. Generally speaking, a north to south, west to east pattern has been followed. In certain cases, particularly those involving one-way-in, same-way-out roads, we have arranged the parks in the order in which they would be encountered on the way into the area, so the standard plan occasionally may be reversed.

State Identifier: The state name and number combination in the upper left corner of each park description provides an easy means of cross-referencing the written information to the numbered locations on the maps in the Appendix.

Park Name: The officially designated name for the park is listed in boldface, followed by the specific category of park in which it is classified by its state. ("State Park", "State Recreation Area", "State Historic Park", and so forth.) In most instances, the park name was transcribed directly from the signpost planted at the park entrance; it may (and often does), vary slightly from the name as it appears in other printed sources, (especially in 'official' park literature). One example: Throughout the West, it's quite common to find places with a 'possessive' noun in their names to be spelled without the possessive apostrophe ("Clarks Camp" vs "Clark's Camp"). We have retained that convention whenever we determined it to be historically appropriate. Evidently, the apostrophe was considered a grammatical frill by many of our forebears.

Larger parks with distinctively different major units may be divided into two or more separate descriptions. For example, if "Canyon River State Park" consists of two large areas, the "Mountain Valley" unit and the "Great Plains" unit, each with different access, facilities, and natural features, the two sections might be titled:

       CANYON RIVER: **CANYON RIVER:**
       MOUNTAIN VALLEY   GREAT PLAINS

Location: This section allows you to obtain a quick approximation of a park's location in relation to nearby key communities, as depicted on the maps in the appendix.

Access: Our *Accurate Access* system makes extensive use of highway mileposts in order to pinpoint the location of access roads, intersections, and other major terminal points. (Mileposts are about 98 percent reliable—but occasionally they are mowed by a snowplow or an errant motorist, and may be missing; or, worse yet, the mileposts were replaced in the wrong spot!) In some instances, locations are noted primarily utilizing mileages between two or more nearby locations—usually communities, but occasionally key junctions or prominent landmarks.

Since everyone won't be approaching a park from the same direction, we've provided access information from two, sometimes three, points. In all cases, we've chosen the access points for their likelihood of use. Distances from communities are listed from the approximate **midtown** point (very often the city hall, couthouse, or post office), unless otherwise specified. Mileages from Interstate highways and other freeway exits are usually given from the approximate center of the interchange. Mileages from access points usually have been rounded to the nearest mile, unless the exact mileage is critical. All instructions are given using the *current official highway map* available free from each state.

Directions are given using a combination of compass and hand headings, i.e., "turn north (left)" or "swing west (right)". This isn't a bonehead navigation system, by any means. When the sun is shining or you're in a region where moss grows on tree trunks, it's easy enough to figure out which way is north. But anyone can become temporarily disoriented on an overcast day or a moonless night while looking for an inconspicuous park turnoff, or while being buzzed by heavy traffic at a key intersection, so we built this redundancy into the system.

Day Use Facilities: Picnic area sizes and number of tables are categorized as: (1) small—up to a dozen; (2) medium—up to 50; (3) large—more than 50. The capacities of parking areas are similarly described. (These are *very* approximate figures because we weren't about to try to *count* all the picnic tables and parking spaces!)

Toilet facilities have been listed thusly: (1) Restrooms—'modern', i.e., flush toilets and usually a wash basin; (2) Vault facilities—'simple', i.e., outhouses, pit toilets, call them what you like. (A rose by any other name.....).

Overnight Facilities: Campgrounds are by far the most common type of overnight facilities offered by state parks. The items in this section have been listed in the approximate order in which a visitor might observe them during a typical swing through a park campground. Following the total number of individual camp units, items pertinent to the campsites themselves are listed, then information related to 'community' facilities. It has been assumed that each campsite has a picnic table.

Site types: (1) Standard—no hookup; (2) Partial hookup—water, electricity; (3) Full hookup—water, electricity, sewer.

We have extensively employed the use of *general* and *relative* terms in describing the size, separation, and levelness of the campsites ("medium to large", "fairly well separated", "basically level", etc.). Please note that "separation" is a measure of relative privacy and is a composite of both natural visual 'screens' and spacing between campsites. The information is presented as an *estimate* by highly experienced observers. Please allow for variations in perception between yourself and the reporters.

Parking Pads: (1) Straight-ins, (sometimes called "back-ins" or "spurs")—the most common type, are just that—straight strips angled off the driveway; (2) Pull-throughs—usually the most convenient type for large rv's, they provide an in-one-end-and-out-the-other parking space; pull-throughs may be either arc-shaped and separated from the main driveway by some sort of barrier or 'island' (usually vegetation), or arranged in parallel rows; (3) Pull-offs—essentially just wide spots adjacent to the driveway. Pad lengths have been categorized as: (1) Short—a single, large vehicle up to about the size of a standard pickup truck; (2) Medium—a single vehicle or combination up to the length of a pickup towing a single-axle trailer; (3) Long—a single vehicle or combo as long as a crew cab pickup towing a double-axle trailer. Normally, any overhang out the back of the pad has been ignored in the estimate, so it might be possible to slip a crew cab pickup hauling a fifth-wheel trailer in tandem with a ski boat into some pads, but we'll leave that to your discretion.

Fire appliances have been categorized in three basic forms: (1) Fireplaces—angular, steel or concrete, ground-level; (2) Fire rings—circular, steel or concrete, ground-level or below ground-level; (3) Barbecue grills—angular steel box, supported by a steel post about 36 inches high. (The trend is toward installing steel fire rings, since they're durable, relatively inexpensive—60 to 80 dollars apiece—and easy to install and maintain. Barbecue grills are often used in areas where ground fires are a problem, as when charcoal-only fires are permitted.)

Certain parks also offer other types of overnight facilties, such as a park-operated lodge, cabins, or group buildings.

Travelers' supply points have been described at five levels: (1) Camper Supplies—buns, beans and beverages; (2) Gas and Groceries—a 'convenience' stop; (3) Limited—at least one store which approximates a small supermarket, more than one fuel station, a general merchandise store, hardware store, and other basic services; (4) Adequate—more than one supermarket, (including something that resembles an IGA or a Safeway), a choice of fuel brands, and several general and specialty stores and services; (5) Complete—they have a major discount store.

♿ Parks reported by state agencies to have facilities for physically challenged persons that conform to the requirements of the Americans with Disabilities Act of 1990 (ADA) have been highlighted with this familiar symbol. In most parks, a minimum you can expect is equal access to restrooms. In many places, special handicapped-access picnic or camp sites, fishing piers and other recreational facilities are also provided, especially in larger parks. Some parks which are not listed as having handicapped access may indeed have some facilities that offer it on a limited basis, usually at restrooms, but they may not technically conform to the rigid standards of the ADA. If you rely on these facilities, it might be a good idea to double check for their existence and condition prior to visiting the park, using the ☎ information.

Park managers, attendants and camp hosts can be expected to be on-site or readily available during the regular season in more than 85 percent of state parks.

Activities & Attractions: As is mentioned a number of times throughout this series, the local scenery may be the principal attraction of the park (and, indeed, may be the *only* one you'll need). Other nearby attractions/activities have been listed if they are low-cost or free, and are available to the general public. An important item: *Swimming and boating areas very often do not have lifeguards.*

Natural Features: Here we've drawn a word picture of the natural environment in and around each park. Please remember that seasonal, even daily, conditions will affect the appearance of the area. A normally "sparkling stream" can be a muddy torrent for a couple of weeks in late spring; a "deep blue lake" might be a nearly empty hole in a drought year; "lush vegetation" may have lost all its greenery by the time you arrive in late October. In the interest of simplicity and easy readability, we list broadleaf trees (i.e., "deciduous" trees, such as cottonwood, maple, oak) as "hardwoods"; cone-bearing needle trees (pines, Western cedar, spruce, etc.) as "conifers". We typically call the relatively small Eastern redcedar and Western junipers "evergreens". This information might be especially helpful to you in determining the amount of shade you can expect to find to help cool you in midsummer. Elevations above 500´ are rounded to the nearest 100´; lower elevations are rounded to the nearest 50´. (Some elevations are estimated, but no one should develop a nosebleed or a headache because of a 100´ difference in altitude.)

Season & Fees: Seasons listed are approximate, since weather conditions, particularly in mountainous or hilly regions, may require adjustments in opening/closing dates. Day use areas are generally available sunrise to sunset; historic sites are typically open during standard business hours; campground entrance gates are usually unlocked from 6:00 a.m. to 10:00 p.m. Fee information listed here and in the Appendix was obtained directly from the responsible agencies a few hours before press time. Fees should be considered *minimum* fees since they are always *subject to adjustment* by agencies or legislatures. Discounts and special passes are usually available for seniors and disabled persons.

Mail & Phone: The exact mailing address of the park is listed, followed by a telephone number which can be called in order to obtain information about current conditions in that park. In the case of 'satellite' or smaller parks, the 'master' park or district office which is listed in this section can be contacted. We've accented the phone number with a ☎ symbol for quick reference. It could be very helpful while you're in a highwayside phone booth fumbling for a quarter or your 'calling card', poking the buttons on the touch-tone pad, and simultaneously trying to hold the handset up to your ear as you're calling a park for reservations, current weather info, or whatever.

Park Notes: Consider this section to be somewhat more subjective in nature than the others. In order to provide our readers with a well-rounded report, we have listed personal comments related to our field observations. (Our enthusiasm for the West is, at times, unabashedly proclaimed. So if the text sometimes reads a bit like a tourist promotion booklet, please bear with us—there's a lot to be enthusiastic about!)

Throughout the series, certain small, relatively undeveloped 'satellite' park areas are given abbreviated 'thumbnail' descriptions in the *Park Notes* section of a principal park. Since these spots often are little-used outback areas, it might pay to check them out if you're in the neighborhood and looking for a simple, tranquil place to sit for a while.

(Indeed, as you read through an occasional marginal park's description, you too may wonder *why* it deserves designation and funding as a state park. In virtually every state, some parks almost certainly have been purchased and/or maintained as a result of local or state political influence—so-called "pork-barrel politics"—rather than for their scenic, recreational or historic value. With all due respect to the noble swine, we privately refer to these as "pork parks" or simply "porkers". In your travels, you too may find a candidate for this special designation.)

Style...

Throughout the *Double Eagle*™ series, we've utilized a free-form writing style. Complete sentences, phrases, and single words have been incorporated into the park descriptions as appropriate under the circumstances. We've adopted this style in order to provide our readers with detailed information about each item, while maintaining conciseness, clarity, and conversationality.

Print...

Another departure from the norm is our use of print sizes which are 20 percent larger (or more) than ordinary guidebooks. We also use more efficient page layouts for less paper waste. It's one thing to read a guidebook in the convenience and comfort of your well-lit living room. It's another matter to peruse the pages while you're bounding and bouncing along in your car or camper as the sun is setting; or by a flickering flashlight inside a breeze-buffeted dome tent. We hope this works for you, too.

Maps...

After extensive tests of the state maps by seasoned travelers, both at home and in the field, we decided to localize all of the maps in one place in the book. Travelers felt that, since pages must be flipped regardless of where the maps are located, it would be more desirable to have them all in one place. We're confident that you'll also find this to be a convenient feature. Likewise, we determined that states should be shown in their entirety, rather than fragmented into regions. Although this makes for 'cramped quarters' in a few high-density recreation areas, map readers preferred the overall 'big picture' approach. Cities shown on the maps are keyed to the cities listed in the *Location* and *Access* sections of the text.

About 'Regs'...

Although this series is about public parks, you'll find comparatively few mentions of rules, regulations, policies, statutes, decrees or dictates. Our editorial policy is simply this: (1) It's the duty of a citizen or a visitor to know his legal responsibilities (and, of course, his corresponding *rights*); (2) Virtually every park has the appropriate regulations publicly posted for all to study; and (3) If you're reading this *Double Eagle*™ Guide, chances are you're in the upper ten percent of the conscientious citizens of the United States or some other civilized country and you probably don't need to be constantly reminded of these matters.

A Final Word...

We've tried very, very hard to provide you with accurate information about the West's great recreation opportunities. But occasionally, all is not as it's supposed to be.....

If a park's access, facilities or fees have been recently changed, please let us know. We'll try to pass along the news to other travelers.

If the persons in the next picnic or camp site flip a frisbee that periodically plops into your potato salad, or keep their generator poppety-popping past midnight so they can cook a turkey in the microwave, blame the bozos, not the book.

If the beasties are a bit bothersome in that beautiful spot down by the bog, note the day's delights and not the difficulties.

Thank you for reading—and using—our book. We hope you'll have many terrific trips!

Arizona State Parks

Patagonia Lake State Park

 *Arizona*

Mojave Desert

Arizona 1 &

LAKE HAVASU:
WINDSOR BEACH
State Park

Location: Western Arizona in Lake Havasu City.

Access: From Arizona State Highway 95 (Lake Havasu Avenue) at milepost 183 +.7 on the north side of Lake Havasu City (1.4 miles north of London Bridge) turn southwest (i.e., left, if you've arrived from the south and just passed London Bridge) onto Industrial Boulevard and proceed 0.5 mile to a fork; take the left fork for 0.15 mile, then turn west (right) to the park entrance station; take the first south (left) turn and continue for 0.7 mile to the campground; or continue ahead for 0.1 mile to the day use area. (A tip on finding the place: the far south end of the park, i.e. the opposite end from the park entrance station, is directly behind the high-rise Holiday Inn.)

Day Use Facilities: Medium-large picnic area; drinking water; restrooms; parking lot.

Overnight Facilities: 74 campsites; (a large group camp is also available, by reservation); sites are medium to large, essentially level, with fair to excellent separation; parking pads are gravel, medium to medium+ straight-ins or long pull-offs or pull-throughs; adequate space for large tents on a sand/gravel surface; fire rings; b-y-o firewood; water at several faucets; restrooms with showers; holding tank disposal station; paved driveways; complete supplies and services are available in Lake Havasu City.

Activities & Attractions: Fishing; boating; boat launches; large, sandy swimming beach; Mojave Sunset Hiking Trail; (a second state park area near Lake Havasu City is at the tip of nearby Pittsburg Point—Site Six has a water safety center, boat launch, restrooms and first aid station); famous relocated London Bridge in Lake Havasu City.

Natural Features: Located on a flat along the west shore of Lake Havasu, a reservoir on the Colorado River, in the Mojave Desert; sites receive minimal to ample shade/shelter from hardwoods and bushes; views of the lake and desert mountains from all picnic sites and many campsites; annual rainfall here is less than 4 inches; posted signs indicate that poisonous snakes and insects inhabit the area; total land area within the entire park is 11,000 acres; elevation 500´.

Season & Fees: Open all year; please see Appendix for standard Arizona state park entry and campground fees.

Mail & Phone: Lake Havasu State Park, 1350 West McCulloch Boulevard, Lake Havasu, AZ 86403; ☎ (928) 855-7851.

Park Notes: The contrast between dozens of square miles of water and hundreds of square miles of rugged mountains is visually powerful and stimulating. Likewise, the contrast between a contemporary desert city and centuries-old London Bridge is curiously appealing. The classic, multi-arched, quarried-stone bridge spans a channel between the mainland and Pittsburg Point. As the story goes, Lake Havasu City's principal real estate developer bought the historic viaduct in 1971 when the City of London was about to scrap it and substitute a modern structure. The bridge was meticulously dismantled stone by stone and each piece was numbered for quick 'n easy reassembly here in the Mojave Desert. (In keeping with the Britannic theme that pervades Lake Havasu City, Windsor Beach was named for England's Royal House of Windsor.)

▲ Arizona 2

LAKE HAVASU:
CATTAIL COVE
State Park

Location: Western Arizona south of Lake Havasu City.

Access: From Arizona State Highway 95 at milepost 167 +.7 (15 miles south of Lake Havasu City, 23 miles north of Parker), turn west onto a paved access road; proceed 0.7 mile west to a fork in the road; take the south (left) fork and go 0.1 mile to the park entrance station; continue ahead for a few yards to the picnic area or 0.1 mile to the campground.

Day Use Facilities: Medium-sized picnic area; drinking water; restrooms; medium-sized parking lot.

Overnight Facilities: 40 campsites, all with partial hookups; sites are rather small, reasonably level, with very little separation; parking pads are sand/gravel, medium to long, straight-ins or parallel pull-throughs; adequate space for large tents; barbecue grills; b-y-o firewood; water at faucets throughout; rest rooms with showers; holding tank disposal station; paved driveways; camper supplies at a nearby marina; complete supplies and services are available in Lake Havasu City.

Activities & Attractions: Boating; excellent boat launch, dock and jetty;

fishing; swimming; playground; horseshoe pits; small amphitheater.

Natural Features: Located on gently sloping terrain above a small cove on the east shore of Lake Havasu, a 25,000-acre lake created on the Colorado River by Parker Dam; campground vegetation consists of some medium to large trees and sparse grass; day use area has a plot of watered, mown lawn; bordered by desert hills and mountains; average high temperatures exceed 100°F June through September; elevation 500´.

Season & Fees: Open all year; please see Appendix for standard Arizona state park entry and campground fees.

Mail & Phone: Lake Havasu State Park, 1350 West McCulloch Boulevard, Lake Havasu, AZ 86403; Cattail Cove local phone ☎ (928) 855-1223.

Park Notes: Cattail Cove is one of only two full-service public campgrounds on this huge lake. (The other public camp is at Windsor Beach; the very large campground and marina right next door to Cattail Cove, at Sand Point, are concession-operated.) Except on holiday weekends, there's *usually* room for late arrivals here. In addition to the two regular public camps, there are more than 200 boat-in primitive campsites, some with vault facilities and ramadas, scattered along the shore of the 45-mile-long lake. The captivatingly bleak terrain around here looks a lot like the land of the Sand People on the desolate planet Tatooine in the film *Star Wars*.

▲ Arizona 3

BUCKSKIN MOUNTAIN:
RIVER ISLAND
State Park

Location: Western Arizona northeast of Parker.

Access: From Arizona State Highway 95 at milepost 156 +.1 (11 miles north of Parker, 2.5 miles south of the settlement of Buckskin, 27 miles south of Lake Havasu City), turn west onto a paved driveway and proceed 0.1 mile to the park.

Day Use Facilities: Group picnic area with ramada; small parking lot.

Overnight Facilities: 30 campsites, including 22 with water hookups; sites are small to small+, level, with very little separation; parking pads are paved, short to medium-length, straight-ins or pull-throughs; some very nice, medium-sized, grassy tent spots; barbecue grills; b-y-o firewood; water at faucets throughout; restrooms with showers; holding tank disposal station; paved driveways; gas and groceries at numerous places north and south of the park; adequate supplies and services are available in Parker.

Activities & Attractions: Boating; boat launch; waterskiing, etc; fishing for largemouth bass, channel cat, crappie and bluegill; Wedge Hill Trail (0.25 mile) leads to an overlook point.

Natural Features: Located in the Mojave Desert on a short, grassy bluff overlooking the Colorado River; mown lawns throughout most of the park area, plus scattered shade trees; jagged rock formations east and north; elevation 450´.

Season & Fees: Open all year; please see Appendix for standard Arizona state park entry and campground fees.

Mail & Phone: Buckskin Mountain State Park, Box BA, Parker, AZ 85344; ☎(928) 667-3231 or ☎(928) 667-3387.

Park Notes: There are some really pleasant little campsites at River Island. This facility is smaller and somewhat less frenetic than its larger sister, Buckskin Point, to the south. Since there are no electrical hookups here, you'll probably find that more small vehicle and/or tent campers favor this unit. Another species of outdoor life-form, the desert bighorn sheep, also favors the Buckskin Mountains, and if you're really lucky you might catch a glimpse of the elusive, sure-footed critter.

▲ **Arizona 4** &

BUCKSKIN MOUNTAIN:
BUCKSKIN POINT
State Park

Location: Western Arizona northeast of Parker.

Access: From Arizona State Highway 95 at milepost 154 +.8 (10 miles north of Parker, 4 miles south of the settlement of Buckskin, 28 miles south of Lake Havasu City), turn west onto a paved access road and proceed 0.1 mile west, then north into the park.

Day Use Facilities: Small picnic area; small parking lot.

Overnight Facilities: 83 campsites in 5 sections, including 48 sites with partial hookups, and 21 sites with electric-only hookups; sites are small to medium-sized and closely spaced; sites 1 to 14 are roomiest, with some separation; parking pads are mostly level, paved, short to medium-length, straight-ins or parking lot spaces; designated, generally excellent, tent-pitching areas on sandy or grassy surfaces; the 21 electric sites have cabanas (upscale sun/wind ramadas that resemble car wash bays); barbecue grills; b-y-o firewood; water at faucets throughout; restrooms with showers; holding tank disposal station; paved driveways; gas and groceries at numerous places north and south of the park; adequate supplies and services are available in Parker.

Activities & Attractions: Boating; boat launch; fishing for largemouth bass, channel cat, crappie and bluegill; waterskiing and other powerboat pursuits; swimming; volleyball court; playground; hiking trails, including the Lightning Bolt Trail (0.5 mile), and the Buckskin Mountain Scenic Trail (2.5 miles), lead through the desert and past old prospecting claims; small visitor center.

Natural Features: Located in the Mohave Desert on the east bank of the Colorado River; vegetation consists of scattered shade trees on watered grass; sandy beach; barren rock hills lie across the river to the west and north, the Buckskin Mountains rise to the east; total park area (including the nearby River Island unit) is 1676 acres; elevation 450´.

Season & Fees: Open all year; please see Appendix for standard Arizona state park entry and campground fees.

Mail & Phone: Buckskin Mountain State Park, Box BA, Parker, AZ 85344; ☎(928) 667-3231 or ☎(928) 667-3387.

Park Notes: There are some really nice campsites at Buckskin Point. A number of them have views of the incredibly blue river. Views of the deep blue Colorado River from the trail overlook points are terrific. Like the other parks along the lower Colorado, it's a paradise for powerboaters and waterskiiers in the hot (110°F) dry summer, and a weekend or week home for Snowbirds and Sunbelt residents during the Mojave's temperate winter.

🔺 Arizona 5

ALAMO LAKE
State Park

Location: West-central Arizona west of Wickenburg.

Access: From U.S. Highway 60 at milepost 61 +.4 in the hamlet of Wenden (11 miles east of Hope, 50 miles west of Wickenburg), turn north onto Alamo Road (paved) and travel 34 miles north and west to the park entrance; 0.2 mile beyond the entrance, turn north (right) onto Cholla Road and proceed 0.7 mile to the C (partial hookup) camping section, and the undeveloped and group camp areas; or continue for 1.4 miles beyond the entrance to the park office; then turn north (right) onto Saguaro Road to the A, B, ramada, and full-hookup camping sections; or stick with the main road for an additional 1.5 miles to the overlook point and day use area. (Note: Contrary to some reports and maps, the above route is the *only* paved access to the park; at least one broken axle on a car-trailer combo has resulted from an excursion on the dirt road from U.S. 93 that's depicted as passable on some maps.)

Day Use Facilities: Small picnic area; vault facilities; small parking lot; concession stand (near the park office).

Overnight Facilities: 131 campsites, including 20 with full hookups and 41 with partial hookups; (a group camp with a ramada and several small, rustic camping cabins are also available); sites are small to medium-sized, with minimal to nominal separation; most parking pads are paved, medium to long straight-ins (many are extra-wide) or pull-offs; a bit of additional leveling will be required in a number of sites; ample space for large tents on a sand/gravel surface; small ramadas (sun shelters) for 12 sites; fire rings or barbecue grills; firewood is usually for sale, or b-y-o; water at several faucets; restrooms with showers; holding tank disposal station; paved driveways; gas and groceries are available in Wenden.

Activities & Attractions: Fishing for bass, catfish, crappie, bluegill; boating; 3 boat launches; rockhounding.

Natural Features: Located on gently sloping desert terrain above Alamo Lake in the Bill Williams River Valley; the lake, a flood control impoundment on the Bill Williams River, has an average maintained surface area of 3500 acres; campsites receive minimal to light shade from small to medium-height hardwoods; views of the lake and of near-distant desert mountains from most sites; park area is 5600 acres; elevation 1200´.

Season & Fees: Open all year; please see Appendix for standard Arizona state park entry and campground fees.

Mail & Phone: Alamo Lake State Park, P.O. Box 38, Wenden, AZ 85357; ☎(928) 669-2088.

Park Notes: Spring and Fall are the most favorable times to come to Alamo Lake. Desert heat discourages summer visits; but the park usually isn't overwhelmingly busy during the relatively mild winter, either. The lake and its associated river system hold the runoff water from a 5000-square-mile chunk of desert that's vulnerable to flash floods. In its relatively brief history, (the dam was completed in 1968) the lake reportedly has risen as much as 11 feet overnight and a total of 100 feet in a season. (Now you know why most of the park's facilities are high up on the slope—it's not just so you'll have a better view!)

▲ Arizona 6 ♿

YUMA TERRITORIAL PRISON
State Historic Park

Location: Southwest corner of Arizona in Yuma.

Access: From Interstate 8 Exit 1 in Yuma (0.5 mile east of the Colorado River bridge), take Giss Parkway for 0.2 mile, then turn north onto Prison Hill Road and proceed 0.4 mile to the park. (Note: I-8 is an east-west highway, but it makes a north-south S-curve as it passes through Yuma; so if you're inbound from Phoenix and points east, at the bottom of the freeway interchange hang a left onto Giss then almost immediately right onto Prison Hill Road; from San Diego, at the bottom of the ramp go right and under the freeway on Giss for a few yards to pick up the prison road.)

Day Use Facilities: Small picnic area with ramada (but are you really sure you want to do lunch here?); drinking water; restrooms; large parking lot.

Overnight Facilities: None; nearest public campground is Squaw Lake (Public Lands/BLM), on the California side of the river, north of Imperial Dam.

Activities & Attractions: Well-preserved structures of the infamous Yuma Prison of the late 1800's and early 1900's; the main gateway, cells and guard tower remain in remarkably good condition; museum with exhibits about 'life' in and around the prison; interpretive programs, tours, slide presentations; group tours are available, by reservation.

Natural Features: Located on a bluff near the east bank of the Colorado River; park area is 9 acres; elevation 150´.

Season & Fees: Open all year, except for a few major holidays (hours may vary and are subject to change); park entry fee $3.00 per person 17 years and older, under 17 free.

Mail & Phone: Yuma Territorial Prison State Historic Park, P.O. Box 10792, Yuma, AZ 85366; ☎(928) 783-4771 (museum) or ☎(928)-343-2500 (office).

Park Notes: Why was Yuma selected as the site of the territorial prison? Probably because they couldn't find any place else that was *worse*. Some literature has likened this hoosegow to the Bastille, but actually it was more like an Old West Sing-Sing. Rather than providing safe keeping for political prisoners, as did the famous French slammer, Yuma Prison was a boarding house for both male and female felons doing hard time for anything from Murder One to purse-snatching. The guest list contains a number of notorious notables, including about 30 women.

Even in the blistering heat of the Yuma summer, the starkly unadorned rock-and-mortar cell blocks *seem* 'stone cold'. It's really eerie within these walls. Once you walk into this place, you'll probably recognize some of its features: quite a few scenes from western films and TV shows have been shot here. Yuma Prison's 'cons' were sent 'up the river', but just *down* the river about a half-mile from the prison is Yuma Crossing (see the following description), another late 1800's state historic site to be checked out while you're in this high-end neighborhood.

▲ Arizona 7

YUMA CROSSING
State Historic Park

Location: Southwest corner of Arizona in Yuma.

Access: From Interstate 8 Exit 1 in Yuma (0.5 mile east of the Colorado River bridge), proceed west on Giss Parkway for 0.6 mile; turn north (right) onto 2nd Avenue, and proceed 0.4 mile to the park.

Day Use Facilities: Small group area; drinking water; restrooms; small parking area.

Overnight Facilities: None; nearest public campground is Squaw Lake (Public Lands/BLM), on the California side of the river, north of Imperial Dam.

Activities & Attractions: Remains of a major military supply point of the late 1800's; interpretive programs.

Natural Features: Located along the east bank of the Colorado River; park area is 10 acres; elevation 150´.

Season & Fees: Open all year, Thursday through Monday, except for a few major holidays (hours may vary and are subject to change); please see Appendix for standard Arizona state park entry fees.

Mail & Phone: Mail c/o Yuma Territorial Prison State Historic Park, P.O. Box 10792, Yuma, AZ 85366; Yuma Crossing phone ☎ (928) 329-0404.

Park Notes: Yuma Quartermaster Depot (QMD for short), was the location of a major military materiel point which supplied army installations in the Southwest as far away as West Texas, from 1864 to 1873. Ships brought the goods up the Gulf of California to the mouth of the Colorado River; the cargos were then loaded onto steamboats and brought up the river to the QMD in Yuma. From here they were dispatched by river steamer or mule train to outposts in five nearby states. As many as 900 mules were corralled on this post, so you can imagine what it must have been like to be a teamster here in the 120°F Yuma summer. Whew! Six of the original structures—the depot office, storehouse, commanding officer's quarters, central kitchen, reservoir, and granary—can be examined at your leisure.

Arizona

Northeast Canyons & High Desert

▲ Arizona 8

RIORDAN
State Historic Park

Location: North-central Arizona in Flagstaff.

Access: From the junction of Interstate Highways 40 & 17 at the south edge of Flagstaff (Exit 195 on I-40, Exit 340 on I-17), proceed north into the city on U.S. Highway 180 (Milton Road) for 1 mile; turn east (right) onto West Chambers Drive and proceed 1 block; turn north (left) onto South Riordan Ranch Road for 1 block, then finally east (right) through the park gateway; the parking lot is at the far east end of the park.

Day Use Facilities: Small picnic area; drinking water and rest rooms inside the visitor center; medium-sized parking lot (limited to vehicles 20´ or less in length); additional, streetside parking is available outside the park.

Overnight Facilities: None; nearest public campgrounds are in Coconino National Forest, in Oak Creek Canyon, along U.S. 89A south of Flagstaff.

Activities & Attractions: Guided tours of the historic Riordan Mansion; (reservations recommended, call the park at the telephone number listed below).

Natural Features: Located in downtown Flagstaff; the park grounds are moderately shaded by tall conifers on a grassy surface; a rail fence borders the mansion, and a chain link security fence or cinder block wall borders the entire park; the heavily timbered San Francisco Peaks rise above 12,600´ north of town; park area is 5 acres; elevation 6900´.

Season & Fees: Open all year, except for a few major holidays; open afternoons only (subject to change); please see Appendix for standard Arizona state park entry fees.

Mail & Phone: Riordan State Historic Park, 1300 South Riordan Ranch Road, Flagstaff, AZ 86001; ☎ (928) 779-4395.

Park Notes: This impressive residence was the home of Michael and Timothy Riordan, a pair of shrewd businessmen who masterminded the success of a Flagstaff-based timber and lumber venture in the early 1900's. The Brothers Riordan married two sisters, Blanche and Caroline, built the mansion in 1904, and the couples settled-in to raise their families in the dual-winged domicile. (The forty-room, 13,000-square foot timber-and-stone duplex was designed by the same architect who engineered the El Tovar Lodge at Grand Canyon.)

You could just come in to wander around the grounds and view this massive log cabin from the outside, but the 'meat and potatoes' of the park are the guided tours of the interior of mansion. All of the furnishings are original, early twentieth century items. (Some of the furniture—for example the kayak-shaped dining table with its peculiar, straight-backed chairs—has an unconventional, almost bizarre, appearance even by 'modern' standards.) Flagstaff has grown up all around this family fortress, and now the neighboring shopping center stands in ironic juxtaposition to the rustic opulence of the house next door.

▲ Arizona 9

SLIDE ROCK
State Park

Location: North-central Arizona south of Flagstaff.

Access: From U.S. Highway 89A at milepost 381 +.2 (6 miles north of the north city limit of Sedona, 17 miles south of Interstate 17 Exit 337 near Flagstaff), turn southwest into the park. (Note: the park entrance is a bit difficult to see as you're approaching it on the narrow, curvy highway, so be watchful; also note that the distance above is listed from Sedona's north city limit rather than the standard midtown point because we're not sure there really *is* a midtown Sedona—the commercial corridor stretches for 4 miles or more along '89A.)

Day Use Facilities: Medium-sized picnic area; drinking water; restrooms; large parking lot.

Overnight Facilities: None; nearest public campgrounds are 5 Coconino National Forest camps on U.S. 89A between milepost 380 and milepost 387.

Activities & Attractions: Swimming, wading, and backside surfing in Oak Creek; wide, paved walkway (0.3 mile) from the parking lot to the slide area; Clifftop hiking trail; birding (a comprehensive bird checklist is available); remains of the early

1900's Pendley homestead, including a house and an apple barn, plus tourist cabins built in 1933; park office is in a restored "Little Brown House" built in 1927; volleyball court; playfield; fishing.

Natural Features: Located on the west bank of Oak Creek (and *in* Oak Creek) in Arizona's scenically renowned Oak Creek Canyon; park vegetation consists of hardwoods along the stream and adjacent slopes, a large open meadow area, and apple orchards which at one time held some 350 trees; picnic sites are lightly shaded; bordered by red-and-white (apples-and-cream?) canyon walls partially topped with hardwoods and conifers; park area is 43 acres; elevation 4900´ to 5100´.

Season & Fees: Open all year; please see Appendix for standard Arizona state park entry fees.

Mail & Phone: Slide Rock State Park, P.O. Box 10358, Sedona, AZ 86336; ☎(928) 282-3034.

Park Notes: Slide Rock's name refers to the recreational side of its trifold personality—the natural 'waterslide' on the solid rock streambed of Oak Creek. The environmentally preferable 'slide' is a 30-foot-long, water-eroded groove in the smooth reddish rock that ends in a shallow pool. The creek is flanked by large, 'table' rocks that make excellent sitting and sunbathing spots. (In warm, sunny weather the rocks make it easier to get toasted evenly on both sides.) The historical aspects of the park are associated with the Pendley homestead, and plans call for restoration of the house and barn through the sale of apples. The apple orchards provide a side benefit: they attract quite an assortment of wildlife, including over 100 species of birds. As for the scenic side of the park.....Oak Creek Canyon, Arizona's second-most popular rift, probably needs no additional words of admiration written on its behalf.

▲ Arizona 10

RED ROCK
State Park

Location: North-central Arizona south of Flagstaff.

Access: From U.S. Highway 89A at a point 3 miles southwest of Sedona, go east on Red Rock Loop Road (Forest Road 216) for 0.5 mile to the park

Day Use Facilities: Small picnic area; drinking water; restrooms; large parking lot.

Overnight Facilities: None; nearest public campgrounds are 5 Coconino National Forest camps on U.S. 89A between milepost 380 and milepost 387, north of Sedona.

Activities & Attractions: Hiking trails; nature trails; fishing.

Natural Features: Located along the banks of Oak Creek just south of Oak Creek Canyon; park vegetation consists of large hardwoods, brush and tall grass; picnic sites are lightly shaded; park area is 290 acres; elevation 4900´.

Season & Fees: Open all year; contact the park office for group reservations; please see Appendix for standard Arizona state park entry fees.

Mail & Phone: Red Rock State Park, P.O. Box 3864, West Sedona, AZ 86340; ☎(928) 282-6907.

Park Notes: Red Rock State Park is undergoing continued development as an environmental education center. It has nearly 300 beautiful acres along the banks of lower Oak Creek. There are some picnicking and hiking opportunities for individuals, but park use is earmarked primarily for "accredited educational groups with an environmental education agenda".

▲ Arizona 11 &

DEAD HORSE RANCH
State Park

Location: Central Arizona southwest of Flagstaff.

Access: From U.S. Highway 89A at milepost 353 in Cottonwood (0.6 mile northwest of the junction of U.S. 89A and Arizona State Highways 260 & 279, 9 miles east of Jerome), travel northwest on Main Street (toward Old Cottonwood and Clarkdale) for 1.8 miles; (Main Street begins as South Main, then becomes North Main and finally East Main as you near the park turnoff); turn northerly onto North Fifth Street and continue for 0.4 mile to a concrete ford across the river; (if you're in a compact car or other low-freeboard vessel, it might be a good idea to size-up the depth of the water and the speed of the current before charging through); cross the stream and continue for another 0.3 mile, then turn east (right) to the park entrance; at a fork just past the entrance station, turn southeast (right) and proceed 0.2 mile to the River area; or take the left fork for 0.05 mile to the large group area, or another 0.15 mile to the campground or a final 0.4 mile to the Lagoon area.

Day Use Facilities: Medium-sized picnic area, large enclosed ramada, drinking water, restrooms and medium-sized parking lot in the River day use area; small picnic area, medium-sized parking lot in the Lagoon day use area; large group ramada (sun shelter) in the group use area (available by reservation).

Overnight Facilities: 45 campsites with partial hookups; (a large group camp/picnic area with a large ramada and several small, rustic camping cabins are also available, by reservation); sites are small to medium-sized, level, with minimal to nominal separation; parking pads are hard-surfaced, short straight-ins, or medium to long, parallel pull-throughs; some good, large, level, grassy tent spots; ramadas (sun shelters) in some sites; barbecue grills; b-y-o firewood; water at sites; restrooms with showers; holding tank disposal station;

paved driveways; adequate+ supplies and services are available in Cottonwood.

Activities & Attractions: Stream and pond fishing; (the "lagoon" is stocked with bass, catfish and panfish, sometimes stocked with trout in winter); hiking and horse trails; nature trail; equestrian facilities in the group area; small visitor center; Tuzigoot National Monument nearby.

Natural Features: Located along the banks of the Verde River in the Verde Valley; park vegetation consists of a variety of smaller trees and bushes, including pines, junipers, mesquite, plus large cottonwoods; River area picnic sites are nicely shaded, Lagoon area picnic sites are minimally shaded; campsites have minimal to light shade; 4-acre impoundment ("lagoon") on the river; some great views of the surrounding mountains, including 7743´ Mingus Mountain to the southwest; park area is 325 acres; elevation 3300´.

Season & Fees: Open all year; please see Appendix for reservation information and standard Arizona state park entry and campground fees.

Mail & Phone: Dead Horse Ranch State Park, P.O. Box 144, Cottonwood, AZ 86326; ☎(928) 634-5283.

Park Notes: Dead Horse Ranch is a bi-seasonal park: it's busy in spring and fall, but not so much so during winter and summer. Apparently a lot of people believe it's a big deal that the summer is a little warm and the winter is a little cool here. That's unfortunate, because it really is a good year 'round park. Good surroundings, both near and far.

🌲 Arizona 12 ♿

JEROME
State Historic Park

Location: Central Arizona northeast of Prescott.

Access: From U.S. Highway 89A at milepost 345 at the lower east end of the city of Jerome (1.1 miles west of the east city limit, 1 mile east of midtown), turn west/northwest onto a paved local road and proceed 1 mile (along the mountainside) to the main parking lot and the museum.

Day Use Facilities: Small picnic area; drinking water and restrooms inside the museum; medium-sized parking lot with limited turnaround space (no trailers); parking for trailers or overflow parking is available in a small/medium-sized lot along the access road just below the park—from there it's a short uphill walk to the museum).

Overnight Facilities: None; nearest public campground is in Dead Horse Ranch State Park.

Activities & Attractions: Museum in the former mansion of copper king James "Rawhide Jimmy" Douglas with displays of old photographs, documents, artifacts, mining machinery, minerals and other memorabilia from the heyday of the copper mining boom town of Jerome; large, three-dimensional scale model of Jerome and its mountaintop perch; orientation video in a screening room with seating; the park is available, by reservation, for meetings, weddings, luncheons and other special events (contact the park office for more information).

Natural Features: Located on a hilltop just below downtown Jerome and overlooking the distant Verde Valley; park grounds are nicely landscaped with mown lawns, mesquite and other hardwoods, and flowers; bordered by semi-arid hills and mountains; elevation 5100´.

Season & Fees: Open all year, except for a few major holidays (hours vary and are subject to change); please see Appendix for standard Arizona state park entry fees.

Mail & Phone: Jerome Historic State Park, Box D, Jerome, AZ 86331; ☎(928) 634-5381.

Park Notes: Jerome is occasionally called "the West's most lively ghost town" or something like that. In the glory days of the late 1800's and early 1900's, it was "the billion dollar copper camp". (The town was named for Eugene Jerome, the principal source of capital for the area's first copper mine.) The park's two-story whitewashed adobe mansion which belonged to "Rawhide

Jimmy" Douglas sits on a hill above the once-famous Little Daisy Mine. A vein of high-grade ore was struck just as copper prices began to skyrocket at the onset of World War I, and Douglas' investment in the Little Daisy paid off in a big way. But the Great Depression, followed by a worldwide decline in copper prices brought the Little Daisy, and eventually all of Jerome's mining, to a halt by the early 1950's. Jerome has been resurrected from obscurity and is now a popular tourist center.

▲ Arizona 13

FORT VERDE
State Historic Park

Location: Central Arizona between Phoenix and Flagstaff.

Access: From Interstate 17 Exit 287 for Cottonwood, Payson, and Camp Verde (53 miles south of Flagstaff, 89 miles north of Phoenix) travel east/southeast on a paved local road for 2.3 miles into Camp Verde; at the corner of Main and Lane Streets on the west edge of town, turn east (left) onto Lane Street and proceed 2 blocks to the park. (Note: Exit 287 is the middle of the three I-17 exits abeam of Camp Verde; you can also take Exit 285 or Exit 289, and then follow local roads into Camp Verde, but the above route is the simplest and probably the quickest, too.)

Day Use Facilities: Small picnic area; drinking water; restrooms; parking in several small areas.

Overnight Facilities: None; nearest public campground is Clear Creek (Coconino National Forest) 7 miles southeast on General Crook Trail.

Activities & Attractions: Visitor center/museum contains a collection of late nineteenth century U.S. Army uniforms, weapons, tack, documents, and communication systems; 4 original, renovated buildings date back to 1873 (Officers' Row tour pamphlet available); parade ground is used periodically for equestrian events.

Natural Features: Located on a hilltop above the Verde Valley; park vegetation consists of a few hardwoods on a surface of sparse grass; picnic tables are lightly shaded; the renovated military buildings are situated on the edge of a several-acre parade ground; park area is 10 acres; bordered by rocky, tree-dotted, semi-arid hills, bluffs and mountains; elevation 3200´.

Season & Fees: Open all year, except for a few major holidays (hours may vary seasonally and are subject to change); please see Appendix for standard Arizona state park entry fees.

Mail & Phone: Fort Verde State Historic Park, P.O. Box 397, Camp Verde, AZ 86322; ☎(928) 567-3275.

Park Notes: Among the biographies-in-brief which are found in the visitor center is one of David White, who served as the base chaplain in the early 1870's. A story is related about the feisty preacher's 'sermon' during an 1866 Sioux attack on a wagon train: "Ladies and Gentlemen. There is a time for praying, and, as we may gather from Holy Writ, a time for fighting. This is a time for fighting." Despite an arrow wound, and armed only with a pistol and a Bible, White led a counterattack against the Indians and later rode through the Sioux forces to get help.

Another exhibit depicts the military heliograph system used in this region. The extensive sun-and-mirror signaling network is said to have been very effective against hostile Apaches and Yavapais who raided local farms and who were the principal reason for the establishment of the fort to begin with. Eventually, some of the Indians themselves took up farming. Fort Verde was finally deactivated in 1890. When you visit the park, be sure to pick up a copy of the Officers' Row pamphlet. It'll provide you with some fresh and frank insights into military life in the nineteenth century.

▲ Arizona 14 ♿

HOMOLOVI RUINS
State Historic Park

Location: Northeast Arizona northeast of Winslow.

Access: From Interstate 40 Exit 257 for Second Mesa/Arizona State Highway 87 (4 miles east of Winslow, 29 miles west of Holbrook), travel north on Highway 87 for 1.2 miles; turn west (left) onto the paved park access road and proceed 1.2 miles to a major 4-way intersection; turn south (left) onto the campground access road and go 0.3 mile to the campground; or continue on the main park road for another 0.5 mile to the visitor center; or go past the visitor center for a final mile to the main day use areas, historical exhibits and the 'dig' areas.

Day Use Facilities: Large picnic area; drinking water; restrooms; parking in several small and medium-sized areas.

Overnight Facilities: 54 campsites; sites are small+, with minimal to nominal separation; parking pads are paved, medium to long, wide straight-ins, or long pull-throughs; a little additional leveling may be required in many sites; adequate room for medium to large tents; ramadas (sun shelters) for all sites; fire rings; b-y-o firewood; water at central faucets; restrooms; showers; holding tank disposal station; paved driveways; complete supplies and services are available in Winslow.

Activities & Attractions: Ruins of a once-large prehistoric Indian community; visitor center (1 mile northwest on the main park road) has interpretive displays; interpretive trails; day use area.

Natural Features: Located hilly terrain on a high desert plain above the Little Colorado River Valley; park vegetation consists mainly of grass and low brush; campsites lack natural shade; distant mountains can be seen to the south, the San Francisco Peaks are in view far to the west; park area is 997 acres; elevation 4900´.

Season & Fees: Open all year; please see Appendix for standard Arizona state park entry and campground fees.

Mail & Phone: Homolovi Ruins State Historic Park, Winslow AZ , ☎(928) 289-4106.

Park Notes: Homolovi Ruins are just that—scattered remnants of six Hopi Indian villages where hundreds, or perhaps several thousand, inhabitants may have set up housekeeping long ago. Some scientific excavation is being conducted, but the vast majority of the archaeological assets preserved in the 1,000-acre park have yet to be unearthed. This park has the largest and probably best-equipped of the camps along I-40 in Arizona. That in itself might induce you to stop here.

▲ Arizona 15 ♿

FOOL HOLLOW LAKE
State Recreation Area/Apache-Sitgreaves NF

Location: Northeast Arizona west of Show Low.

Access: From Arizona State Highway 260 at milepost 338 (3 miles west/northwest of Show Low) turn east (i.e., right, if approaching from Show Low) onto Old Linden Road West and proceed 0.6 mile; turn north (left, just past 32nd Street North) onto a recreation area access road and proceed 1.5 miles north/northeast to the campground.

Day Use Facilities: Several small and medium-sized picnic areas; group picnic areas with shelters; drinking water; restrooms; medium-sized and large parking areas.

Overnight Facilities: 123 campsites, many with partial hookups; (a group camp is planned); sites are small+ to medium-sized, adequately level, with nominal to fair separation; parking pads are hard-surfaced, medium to long straight-ins or pull-throughs; designated tent areas; fire rings; b-y-o firewood is suggested; water near each site; restrooms; showers; holding tank disposal station; (sewer hookups may be available in the future); paved driveways; complete supplies and services are available in Show Low.

Activities & Attractions: Fishing for trout, bass, walleye, crappie, channel cat;

boating; boat launches and docks; hiking trails; amphitheater; cable TV; playground; visitor center; interpretive programs.

Natural Features: Located on gently rolling terrain on the northeast shore of Fool Hollow Lake in the White Mountains; vegetation consists of light to medium-dense ponderosa and piñon pines, plus some junipers and oaks; a number of artificial islands have been built to attract wildlife; encircled by conifer-covered hills; elevation 6300´.

Season & Fees: April to October; please see Appendix for standard Arizona state park fees; 14 day camping limit; jointly administered and operated by Arizona State Parks and Apache-Sitgreaves National Forests.

Mail & Phone: Fool Hollow Lake Recreation Area, c/o Lakeside Ranger District, Apache-Sitgreaves NF, RR3 Box B-50 Pinetop-Lakeside AZ 85929; park phone ☎(928) 537-3680.

Park Notes: Formerly little more than a pleasant jackcamping spot, Fool Hollow Lake has undergone a major, megabuck metamorphosis. According to local official sources, a collaboration of a dozen federal, state, local and private entities, including U.S. senators and congressmen, planned this ultra-modern undertaking. Somewhere in the neighborhood of $10 million may eventually be spent in developing this formerly tranquil national forest neighborhood just outside of town. Some campers who support simpler campstyles argue that the same number of government greenbacks could have been used to improve or construct several less-opulent recreation areas in more diverse locations. ($10 million doesn't buy as many barrels of salt pork as it once did. Perhaps the decision to retain the original name of the place has its merits.)

🔺 **Arizona 16**

LYMAN LAKE
State Park

Location: Eastern Arizona north of Springerville.

Access: From U.S. Highways 180 & 666 at Highway 180 milepost 380 + .4 (20 miles north of Springerville, 10 miles south of St. Johns), turn east onto Arizona State Highway 81 and proceed 1.6 miles to the park entrance station; continue ahead for 0.2 mile to the day use area, or south (right) to the campground, 0.1 mile beyond the entrance.

Day Use Facilities: Large picnic area with several small ramadas; large ramada (reservable by groups); drinking water; restrooms; large parking area; concession stand.

Overnight Facilities: 61 sites, including 25 with partial hookups, in 2 sections; (a group camp with a meeting hall and several small, rustic camping cabins and yurts are also available, by reservation); sites are small to medium-sized, with minimal separation; parking pads are paved, medium to long straight-ins or pull-throughs; a minor amount of additional leveling may be needed in some sites; many large, grassy tent areas; many sites have ramadas (sun/partial wind shelters); barbecue grills and fire rings; b-y-o firewood; water at faucets throughout; restrooms with showers; holding tank disposal station; paved driveways; adequate supplies and services are available in St. Johns and Springerville.

Activities & Attractions: Boating; boat launch and dock; fishing for walleye, northern pike, largemouth bass, catfish and crappie; designated swimming area; Indian petroglyphs; interpretive programs in summer; several short hiking trails; volleyball court.

Natural Features: Located on a gentle slope above the west shore of 1500-acre Lyman Lake, an irrigation impoundment on the Little Colorado River; planted hardwoods provide minimal to light natural shade/shelter in some sites; surrounded by dry, colorful bluffs and hills dotted with trees and brush, and rolling plains; typically windy; park area is 1180 acres; elevation 6000´.

Season & Fees: Open all year; please see Appendix for reservation information, and standard Arizona state park entry and campground fees.

Mail & Phone: Lyman Lake State Park, P.O. Box 1428, St. Johns, AZ 85936; ☎(928) 337-4441.

Park Notes: Even at 6000´, summer days here are typically in the 80's and lower 90's. Best times to visit are late spring and early fall, (avoid summer holiday weekends.) It might be noted that, although the facilities are available year 'round, the cold, blustery winter weather at this altitude isn't exactly conducive to January cook-outs or lengthy camp-outs. Lyman Lake is really a good-sized body of water for this part of the country, although it is fairly shallow— the deepest trough is 45 feet, and the average depth is closer to 30-35 feet. Most of the lake is available to just about any type of water-based activity, but the west end is designated as a no-wake zone in order to prevent waterskiers and speedboaters from tangling with fishermen. (The west end, which is near the dam, has a deep, sharply contoured bottom and looks like it might be one of the best fishing spots.) All picnic and camp sites have lake views.

 Arizona ⚑

Southeast Sonoran Desert

🌲 **Arizona 17** ♿

LOST DUTCHMAN
State Park

Location: Central Arizona east of Phoenix.

Access: From Arizona State Highway 88 at milepost 201 +.1 (5 miles northeast of Apache Junction, 12 miles southwest of Tortilla Flat), turn southeast onto a gravel access road and proceed 0.1 mile to the park entrance station; continue ahead for 0.1 mile, then turn southwest (right) for 0.7 mile to the campground; or continue east/southeast past the campground turnoff for 0.2 mile to the day use area.

Day Use Facilities: Medium-sized picnic area with a dozen small ramadas (sun shelters) and 2 group ramadas; (a group area with 1 medium-sized ramada and several small ramadas is available by reservation); drinking water; restrooms;

several small and medium-sized parking lots.

Overnight Facilities: 35 campsites in 3 small loops within an oval driveway; (a group camp is also available for groups with self-contained rv's, by reservation only); sites are generally medium to large, level, and reasonably well separated; parking pads are gravel, medium to long, straight-ins or pull-throughs; most of the pads and driveways are rock-bordered; large tent spots; barbecue grills; b-y-o charcoal; water at central faucets; restrooms; holding tank disposal station; gravel driveways; adequate+ supplies and services are available in Apache Junction.

Activities & Attractions: Hiking and interpretive trails through the park: Discovery Trail (0.6 mile) and Native Plant Trail (0.25 mile); hiking trails into adjacent Tonto National Forest and the Superstition Wilderness: Treasure Loop Trail (2.4 miles), Siphon Draw Trail (1.6 miles), Prospector's View Trail, (0.7 mile), and Jacob's Crosscut Trail (0.85 mile); guided hikes and campfire programs, October to April; boating and swimming on Canyon Lake, 10 miles east.

Natural Features: Located on a desert plain at the north/west base of the Superstition Mountains; classic desert environment includes sandy/rocky soil, saguaro, cholla and barrel cactus, creosote bush and mesquite; summer daytime temperatures consistently exceed 110°F; winter highs are typically in the 60's; park area is 292 acres; elevation 1800´.

Season & Fees: Open all year; please see Appendix for standard Arizona state park entry and campground fees.

Mail & Phone: Lost Dutchman State Park, 6109 North Apache Trail, Apache Junction, AZ 85219; ☎(480) 982-4485.

Park Notes: The legend of the Lost Dutchman Mine goes back to the 1840's when a prominent Mexican family named Peralta reportedly operated a highly profitable gold mine in the Superstition Mountains and hauled the gold back across the border. The mine was abandoned in the late 1840's after the Apaches bushwhacked a Peralta pack train toting gold to Mexico.

The location of the diggings remained a mystery until some time in the 1870's when, as the story goes, the "Dutchman", a German immigrant named Jacob Waltz, rediscovered the mine and worked it with his partner, Jacob Weiser. Stories circulated that the pair had stashed their newly acquired assets in several spots in the Superstitions. After Weiser was dispatched by an Apache bullet (or, as some say, by lead from his amigo's .44), Waltz left the mountains, never to return.

Before his death in 1891, the Dutchman supposedly disclosed the whereabouts of the mine to a woman who had taken care of him in his final years. But neither she, nor any of the countless other searchers, has ever been able to find the Dutchman's lost treasure. Stories about frustrated seekers of the grand prize of the Superstitions, some of them laced with intrigue and death, continue even now. (Didn't Ronald Reagan star in one of those old *Death Valley Days* episodes about the Lost Dutchman?)

▲ Arizona 18 ♿

BOYCE THOMPSON SOUTHWESTERN ARBORETUM
State Park & Research Area

Location: Central Arizona west of Superior.

Access: From U.S. Highway 60 at milepost 223 (4 miles west of Superior, 11 miles east of Florence Junction), turn south into the park; upper parking lot is just off the highway; lower parking lot is several yards past the upper lot, south of the visitor center.

Day Use Facilities: Medium-sized picnic area; drinking water; restrooms; 2 large parking lots.

Overnight Facilities: None; nearest public campground is Oak Flat (Tonto National Forest) 5 miles east of Superior, (no drinking water at Oak Flat).

Activities & Attractions: Self-guiding trails through desert gardens; (wheelchair-handicapped access on the main loop trail goes only about a quarter-mile, as far as

Ayer Lake, then the trail becomes narrow, steep and rough); informational ramadas; visitor center; greenhouses; remains of a desert homesteader's small house; special events, lectures, and workshops are held throughout the year (please contact the park for a current schedule).

Natural Features: Located amid high desert hills and mountains; the arboretum is landscaped with one of the largest assortments of cacti, palms and other desert vegetation from North America, and trees and shrubs from desert regions on other continents; herb garden; Queen Creek flows (seasonally) along the south and east sides of the park; Ayer Lake is a small impoundment which serves as a watering hole for the park's resident critters (the list includes plenty of birds and small mammals, lots of little lizards, plus snakes, and even shy Gila Monsters); picnic sites are very nicely shaded; total park area is 420 acres; elevation 2400´.

Season & Fees: Open all year, except for a few major holidays (hours may vary seasonally and are subject to change); park entry fees: $4.00 for ages 13 years and older, $2.00 for ages 5-12, under 5 free (subject to change); (pets are OK, if they're on a short leash).

Mail & Phone: Boyce Thompson Southwestern Arboretum, P.O. Box AB, Superior, AZ 85273; ☎(520) 689-2811.

Park Notes: Until you actually walk the trails of this mountain masterpiece, you may not be able to imagine the fabulous variety of desert flora that's been planted and cared for here. Given a choice, most people would visit in spring, when the brilliant blooms of the cacti brighten up the grounds; but even in midsummer plenty of shade makes the place highly hospitable. (Nevertheless, a hat, mantilla or umbrella is still standard equipment for summer visitors; drinking water is available at several points.) The self-guiding main loop trail is about 1.25 miles long and encircles rocky Magma Ridge; the trail is generously shaded over much of its length.

In addition to the sections of native vegetation, the cactus garden, eucalyptus, boojums, and exotic shrubs and trees along the trail, you can also pay a visit to the Clevenger house. The original homesteaders of what is now the arboretum land was a family of five who built a tiny, stone-and-adobe, slant-roofed house against the vertical rock wall of Magma Ridge. (The cliff serves as the natural fourth wall of the house.) William Boyce Thompson bought the Clevenger place in the early 1920's and developed it as a delightful and practical desert garden. The arboretum is now cooperatively managed by a private-public coalition made up of the not-for-profit arboretum corporation, the state parks department and the University of Arizona. This super place is near the top of the Arizona "Definitely Worth The Trip" list.

🌲 Arizona 19

McFARLAND
State Historic Park

Location: Central Arizona northeast of Casa Grande.

Access: From U.S. Highway 89 (Pinal Parkway) at milepost 134 +.6 in Florence, turn west onto Ruggles Avenue and proceed 0.5 mile; the park is located on the northwest corner of the intersection of Ruggles Avenue and Main Street.

Day Use Facilities: Small picnic area; drinking water and restrooms inside the museum; medium-sized parking lot (including enough space for a few large rv spaces) on the west side of the museum; additional streetside parking is available.

Overnight Facilities: None; nearest public campgrounds are in Catalina and Picacho Peak State Parks.

Activities & Attractions: First Pinal County Courthouse, now a museum with exhibits and memorabilia of Governor Ernest W. McFarland, and local historical information.

Natural Features: Located on a desert plain; the park grounds are lightly to moderately shaded by large hardwoods; park area is 2 acres; elevation 1200´.

Season & Fees: Open all year, Thursday through Monday, except for a few major

holidays (hours may vary seasonally and are subject to change); please see Appendix for standard Arizona state park entry fees.

Mail & Phone: McFarland State Historic Park, Box 109, Florence, AZ 85232; ☎(520) 868-5216.

Park Notes: The renovated, single-story adobe museum building was designed in an unpretentious, practical and yet classically handsome architectual style which could be termed 'Anglo-Sonoran'. It served as the original Pinal County Courthouse from 1878 until 1891, when a much more elaborate, Victorian-style courthouse was built to replace it. (The second home of county government has since been supplanted by a third building with contemporary styling.) The first courthouse then went through a succession of terms as county hospital, welfare and public health center, home for the elderly, and a local museum until it was purchased by former Governor Ernest McFarland and his wife Edna in 1974. The McFarlands then deeded the property to the state. Known to his constituents as just "Mac", McFarland's political career spanned four decades: county attorney, superior court judge, U.S. senator and senate majority leader, Arizona governor, and State Supreme Court justice. Museum exhibits now principally present McFarland's governmental documents and memorabilia; a replica of an early courtroom and other items related to local history are also featured.

🌲 Arizona 20

PICACHO PEAK
State Park

Location: South-central Arizona between Casa Grande and Tucson.

Access: From Interstate 10 Exit 219 for Picacho Peak Road (25 miles southwest of Casa Grande, 40 miles northwest of Tucson), turn west off the freeway; proceed west for 0.5 mile on Picacho Peak Road (paved) to the park entrance/office; a day use area and the main (full service) campground are south (left) of the park entrance; or continue ahead (west) past the entrance for 0.5 mile to 1 mile to additional day use areas along the main park road and in side loops; or continue even farther west and southwest for another mile to the new campground, groups camps, equestrian parking lot and hikers' parking lot.

Day Use Facilities: 5 small picnic areas, several with medium-sized ramadas (sun shelters); drinking water; restrooms; several small and medium-sized parking areas.

Overnight Facilities: *Main campground*: 35 campsites, including many with partial hookups, and 7 designated tent units; most sites are situated in a paved parking lot arrangement, with tables around the perimeter; sites are small, basically level, with nil separation; parking spaces are short to medium-length straight-ins or pull-offs; enough space for a small tent on a rocky surface in the tent sites; fireplaces; b-y-o firewood; water at sites with hookups, plus central faucets; restrooms with showers.

New campground: 92 campsites in 3 loops; (2 group camps are also available, by reservation); sites are small to medium-sized, with minimal separation; parking pads are paved, long straight-ins or pull-throughs; a touch of additional leveling might be required in some sites; paved driveways; (note: in the early stages of development, the new campground will serve self-contained rv campers only; reportedly, campsite utilities, restrooms and other facilities will be installed, contingent upon available funds); gas and camper supplies at freeway exits in the vicinity; nearest source of complete supplies and services is Casa Grande.

Activities & Attractions: Nature trail; hiking trails, including the 2-mile Hunter Trail to the summit of Picacho Peak and the less-strenuous 0.7-mile Calloway Trail; trail to children's cave (a 7´ x 8´ x 15´ erosion feature on the mountainside that hardly any nook-loving kid could pass up); playground; small amphitheater; parking lots for hikers and equestrians.

Natural Features: Located on a slope near the base of 3374´ Picacho Peak; park vegetation consists of a broad assortment of cactus and other typical desert plants; park area is 3400 acres; elevation 1900´ to 3400´.

Season & Fees: Open all year; please see Appendix for reservation information and standard Arizona state park entry and campground fees.

Mail & Phone: Picacho Peak State Park, P.O. Box 275, Picacho, AZ 85241; ☎ (520) 466-3183.

Park Notes: Picacho Peak has been used as a landmark by desert travelers since the days of the Spanish explorers. As you approach the park on the Interstate you'll probably be able to fairly easily pick it out from the other, 'ordinary' desert mountains in this area. Look for a complex peak with a pair of 'ears', or a peak which resembles the 'buckhorn' notch on the rear sight of a rifle. (Or does it suggest a hen sitting on her nest?) Once you're in the park you'll begin to really appreciate what is literally a forest of saguaro and other cacti which cover the lower slopes of the mountain. This is probably the handiest state park for interstate highway travelers in all of Arizona.

🏕 **Arizona 21** ♿

CATALINA
State Park

Location: Southern Arizona north of Tucson.

Access: From U.S. Highway 89 at milepost 81 +.1 (14 miles north of downtown Tucson, 10 miles south of the junction of U.S. Highway 89 and Arizona State Highway 77 at Oracle Junction north of Catalina), turn east into the park entrance, (it would be difficult to miss this park entrance); proceed 0.4 mile to the entrance station; proceed east for 0.4 mile, then turn north (left) for 0.2 mile, then east (right) into the campground; or continue east on the main park road for another 0.1 to 0.5 mile to the day use and group use areas, all on the north side of the road; or go past the day use areas for a final 0.5 to 0.7 mile to the trailhead parking lots and a turnaround loop at the end of the park road. (Total distance from the main highway to the turnaround loop is 2.0 miles.)

Day Use Facilities: Large day use area which includes a dozen small picnic areas and 2 medium-sized group use areas; (group areas are available by reservation only, contact the park office); drinking water; restrooms, plus auxiliary vault facilities; several medium to large parking lots.

Overnight Facilities: 50 campsites in 2 loops; (in addition, the 2 group areas are reservable for camping); sites are large, level, with fair to good separation; parking pads are paved, long straight-ins or super long pull-throughs; very large tent areas; barbecue grills (charcoal fires only permitted); water at several faucets; restrooms with showers; holding tank disposal station; paved driveways; complete supplies and services are available on the north edge of Tucson, 6 miles south.

Activities & Attractions: 2 hiking/equestrian trails; nature trail and birding trail; equestrian facilities and bridal trail; trailhead parking; trails lead into adjacent Coronado National Forest.

Natural Features: Located on a desert plain at the northwest corner of the rocky Santa Catalina Mountains; vegetation consists of good-sized trees and brush which provide minimal to light shade/shelter in most picnic and camp sites, plus varieties of typical smaller desert plants; park area is 5500 acres; elevation 2700´ to 3000´.

Season & Fees: Open all year; please see Appendix for reservation information standard Arizona state park entry and campground fees.

Mail & Phone: Catalina State Park, P.O. Box 36986, Tucson, AZ 85740; ☎(520) 628-5798.

Park Notes: Except for the campground, (which, even without hookups, is still fairly well developed), the park maintains a natural atmosphere. If you arrive from the north on a typical day, it might be a touch difficult to believe that one of the Southwest's largest cities is just 'right over the next hill' from the park. Another nearby state park area, accessed from State Highway 77 northeast of Catalina, is undergoing development and will be available to individuals on a limited basis. Oracle State Park, off the Old Mount Lemmon Road, 1 mile east of the town of Oracle, is being developed as an environmental education center. The park's buildings and its 4000 acres in the high desert hills northeast of the Santa Catalina Mountains have been reserved for nature study, hiking and picnicking by day visitors and by accredited educational groups. It is suggested that you contact the state parks office in Phoenix or the Oracle State Park office (602-896-2425) for information about the park's availability.

🌲 **Arizona 22**

ROPER LAKE
State Park

Location: Southeast Arizona south of Safford.

Access: From U.S. Highway 666 at milepost 115 +.7 (5 miles south of Safford, 2 miles north of the junction of U.S. 666 & Arizona State Highway 366, 29 miles north of Interstate 10 Exits 252 & 255), turn east onto Roper Lake Road (paved), proceed 0.5 mile, then turn south (right) for 0.1 mile to the park entrance station; just past the entrance, turn left, and proceed 0.6 mile to the campsites and boat launch on the east side of the lake; or turn right, and follow the park road for 0.6 mile around to the day use and camping areas on the south side of the lake. **Additional Access:** for the Dankworth Ponds unit: from U.S. 666 near milepost 113 (8 miles south of Safford), turn east onto a park access road and proceed 0.6 mile to the park entrance.

Day Use Facilities: Medium-sized picnic area with about a dozen small ramadas (sun shelters), large ramada (reservable by groups); (small, rustic camping cabins are also available, by reservation); drinking water, restrooms, and large parking lot in the main park; medium-sized picnic area with several small ramadas, drinking water, restrooms and medium-sized parking lot in the Dankworth Ponds unit.

Overnight Facilities: 24 campsites; (a group camp area is also available, by reservation); sites are small to medium-sized, essentially level, with minimal to nominal separation; most parking pads are short to medium-length, straight-ins or pull-offs; some excellent tent spots; some sites have small ramadas (sun shelters); assorted fire appliances; b-y-o firewood; water at several faucets; restrooms with showers; holding tank disposal station; paved or gravel driveways; adequate supplies and services are available in Safford.

Activities & Attractions: Fishing for stocked bass, bluegill, crappie and catfish; fishing piers; limited boating (no gasoline motors); boat launch and docks; windsurfing; swimming beach; 'hot tub' (a rock-lined pool filled by hot springs); Mariah Mesa Nature Trail (0.75 mile loop).

Natural Features: Located along the shore of 33-acre Roper Lake; planted hardwoods, palms and grass augment natural, desert vegetation; day use area is on a long peninsula which juts out from the south shore past the mid-lake point; campsites are along or near the shore; surrounding countryside is desert ringed by mountains; the rugged Pinaleno Mountains, including 10,700´ Mount Graham, rise to the west; total park area is 319 acres; elevation 3100´.

Season & Fees: Open all year; please see Appendix for reservation information and standard Arizona state park entry and campground fees.

Mail & Phone: Roper Lake State Park, Route 2, Box 712, Safford, AZ 85546; ☎(928) 428-6760.

Park Notes: This is an attractive little lake, especially for this part of the country. Many of the most picnic sites and many of the campsites have excellent views. Some campsites provide tentside fishing. The busy season at Roper Lake is March to October. Even at a relatively high elevation of 3100´, it still gets quite warm in midsummer around here, but any wet spot in Southeast Arizona will draw a crowd.

🌲 **Arizona 23** ♿

TUBAC PRESIDIO
State Historic Park

Location: Southern Arizona north of Nogales.

Access: From Interstate 19 Exit 34 for Tubac (34 km/21 miles north of Nogales, 65 km/40 miles south of Tucson), proceed to the east side of the Interstate to a 'T' intersection, then north on a frontage road for 0.45 mile; turn east (right), then immediately swing south (right again) and follow Tubac Road for 0.25 mile as it curves from south to east through the small central business district to the east end of town; jog south (right) then east (left) onto Presidio Drive for a final 0.15 mile to the park.

Day Use Facilities: Small picnic area; drinking water; restrooms; medium-sized parking lot.

Overnight Facilities: None; nearest public campground is Peña Blanca (Coronado National Forest) on State Highway 289 northwest of Nogales.

Activities & Attractions: Visitor center with informational displays and artifacts; archaeological 'dig' of the presidio's original foundation and walls, a few yards west of the museum.

Natural Features: Located on the edge of a desert plain in the Santa Cruz Valley; the museum grounds are nicely landscaped in the typical Southwest style; picnic sites are very lightly shaded by mesquite; bordered by desert mountains east and west; park area is 10 acres; elevation 3500´.

Season & Fees: Open all year, except for a few major holidays (hours may vary seasonally and are subject to change); please see Appendix for standard Arizona state park entry fees.

Mail & Phone: Tubac Presidio State Historic Park, Box 1296, Tubac, AZ 85646; ☎(520) 398-2252.

Park Notes: Quite a bit of significant Western history and several 'firsts' have sprung from this little spot. The Presidio de San Ignacio de Tubac was garrisoned by the Spanish in June 1752 and was the first town established in Arizona by Europeans. It was from this fort that the famous Southwest explorer, Juan Bautista de Anza, commanded an expedition to California that led to the founding of San Francisco in 1776. As a result of the Gadsden Purchase in 1853, in which the United States rounded out its present southern boundary by buying a relatively small strip of Arizona real estate from Mexico, Tubac was brought under the Stars and Stripes. Arizona's first newspaper, *The Weekly Arizonian*, was published here on March 3, 1859. By the beginning of the War Between the States in 1860, Tubac was the largest town in Arizona. But troops which protected settlers from the Apaches were needed elsewhere for the war effort. Residents quickly departed, and Tubac became another Arizona ghost town (although it has recently been somewhat revitalized as an artists' haven and tourist center). In 1959, Arizona's first state park was established here.

▲ **Arizona 24**

PATAGONIA LAKE
State Park

Location: Southern Arizona northeast of Nogales.

Access: From Arizona State Highway 82 at milepost 12 +.1 (12 miles northeast of Nogales, 7 miles southwest of Patagonia), turn west onto a paved access road and travel 4 miles west and north to the park entrance station; continue ahead for 0.1 mile to a 'T' intersection; turn west (left) and proceed 0.1 mile to the main camping area, or 0.4 mile to the west day use area; alternately, turn east (right) at the 'T' and proceed 0.1 mile to the Boulder Beach area or 0.2 mile to the east camping areas (including the hookup sites).

Day Use Facilities: Large picnic area with about 20 small ramadas and a medium-sized group ramada at the west end of the park; (large ramada is reservable by groups, contact the park office); medium-sized picnic area with a few small ramadas and a medium-sized ramada at Boulder Beach; drinking water; restrooms; large and medium-sized parking lots.

Overnight Facilities: 105 campsites, including 10 with partial hookups, in 2 sections; (12 boat-in campsites, mostly along the north shore, are also available); sites are small to medium-sized, with

minimal to nominal separation; most parking pads are hard-surfaced, medium to long straight-ins, and some are extra wide; parking pads in the main area are basically level, but some pads in the more hilly east area may need additional leveling; medium to large tent areas; fireplaces; b-y-o firewood; water at several faucets; restrooms with showers; paved driveways; camper supplies on the premises; gas and groceries in Patagonia; complete supplies and services are available in Nogales.

Activities & Attractions: Boating; boat launch and dock; marina; fishing for bass, catfish, crappie, bluegill, plus stocked trout in winter); long, grassy swimming beach; long, arched foot bridge over the narrow mouth of a bay links the main campground and the west day use area; 1-mile-long Sonoita Creek Trail follows the southeast shore to the lake's inlet.

Natural Features: Located on the east shore of 2.5-mile-long, 265-acre Patagonia Lake; picnic and camp sites receive very light to light shade/shelter from small to medium-sized hardwoods, plus a few pines and junipers/cedars; most picnic sites in the west area are walk-ins which are situated around a hillside; surrounded by hills covered with grass and dotted with trees, brush and ocotillo, and distant desert mountains; park area is 640 acres; elevation 3800´.

Season & Fees: Open all year; please see Appendix for reservation information and standard Arizona state park entry and campground fees.

Mail & Phone: Patagonia Lake State Park, P.O. Box 274, Patagonia, AZ 85624; ☎(520) 287-6965.

Park Notes: The park is situated at about the midpoint on the lake's south shore at the narrowest segment of the main body of the lake. A dozen arms and bays and coves make life interesting for boaters and shore-following hikers. A unique feature of this park is the footbridge which spans the entrance to the bay—there's nothing like it anywhere else in the West. Most picnic sites and some campsites, although not right on the lake shore, are just above the lake, so the views are pretty respectable. Suggestion:

check out the west day use area for a picnic spot, or the smaller section east of the main camping area for a campsite, if you prefer a little less local activity, a little more privacy and somewhat better views. Weekends are busy throughout the year in this park, partly because of the temperate climate at this altitude-and-latitude combination. When you visit here, you'll see another reason for the park's popularity: this is one of the prettiest areas in Southern Arizona. Patagonia takes its name from the isolated, and only recently explored region near the southern tip of South America just north of Tierra del Fuego. Appropriate.

▲ Arizona 25

TOMBSTONE COURTHOUSE
State Historic Park

Location: Southeast Arizona in Tombstone.

Access: From U.S. Highway 80 (Fremont Street) at milepost 317 +.2 at the intersection of Fremont and Third Streets in Tombstone, (a couple of blocks west/northwest of the midtown point and the pedestrian 'skyway' which spans the main drag), turn southerly (i.e., right, if approaching from Benson and Interstate 10) onto Third Street and proceed 2 blocks; the courthouse is at the corner of Third and Toughnut.

Day Use Facilities: Small picnic area across the street; drinking water and restrooms inside the courthouse; small parking lot and streetside parking, adjacent; book/gift shop inside the museum.

Overnight Facilities: None; nearest public campground is Cochise Stronghold (Coronado National Forest), 9 miles west of the community of Sunsites.

Activities & Attractions: Original Cochise County Courthouse which now serves as a museum featuring informational displays and exhibits about frontier life in and around Old Tombstone.

Natural Features: Located in-town surrounded by a brushy plain bordered by high-desert hills and mountains; the courthouse is flanked by tall hardwoods;

picnic site is very lightly shaded; elevation 4500´.

Season & Fees: Open all year, except for a few major holidays (hours may vary seasonally and are subject to change); please see Appendix for standard Arizona state park entry fees.

Mail & Phone: Tombstone Courthouse State Park, Box 216, Tombstone, AZ 85638; ☎ (520) 457-3311.

Park Notes: Tombstone—"The Town Too Tough To Die"—began as a mining camp founded in 1879 by prospector Ed Schieffelin. As the story goes, Schieffelin had received a friendly warning from his buddies that the only thing he would find here in Apache country would be his own tombstone. After he struck paydirt in the nearby silver-rich hills, the town which sprang up on this spot was named Tombstone as a good-natured tribute to Schieffelin's tenacity. By 1881, the town's population had reached 10,000, and it was named the county seat of Cochise County. A year later, the victorian-style, cupola-topped courthouse was built. Tombstone's glory lasted only a few years, and it was all but over by the late 1880's as the mines became unworkable because of persistent flooding. In 1929, the county seat was moved to Bisbee, and the old courthouse was basically abandoned until it was resurrected as a museum in the 1950's.

Most of the displays inside the present state park feature information and materials from Tombstone's Old West heyday. Downstairs, the self-guided tour begins in the sheriff's office, which is next to a room featuring information about some of the famous people and events of Tombstone: The Gunfight at the OK Corral (which, according to some historians, didn't actually take place at the OK Corral); Wyatt Earp and his brothers; the Earps' arch enemies, the Clantons; tough lawman John Slaughter; and of course John Henry "Doc" Holliday, and Doc's girlfriend Kate Fisher, known far and wide as "Big Nose Kate". (Gunfighter Holliday was a professional dentist, but most historians agree that he squeezed a trigger more often than he yanked a tooth.) A mining room and an 'amusement' parlor round out the main floor presentation.

The courtroom on the second floor—with its judicial bench, seating for the Group of Twelve Peers, rows of wooden 'pews' for spectators, and a pot-bellied stove—is right out of a Hollywood western movie. Just outside the courtroom is the county attorney's office. The Cattlemen's corner has a number of saddles and tack and other riding gear, a hundred different samples of barbed wire, and information about the local environment. And the Pioneers room contains first-rate displays of clothing, pewter, English china and other fineries. Lots of neat things throughout the building.

Nowadays, Tombstone owes most of its livelihood to tourism, and in addition to visiting the state park, you can 'mosey on down' to Allen Street to complete your visit. A couple-dozen strictly Old West shops, saloons and cafes line the narrow street and provide the proper frontier ambience. It's just around the corner from the town's historic newspaper, the *Tombstone Epitaph*, and a couple of blocks from Boothill Cemetery with its own unique collection of epitaphs. Is all of this a tad touristy? Maybe. But it's still fun.

▲ Arizona 26 ♿

KARTCHNER CAVERNS
State Park

Location: Southeast Arizona southeast of Tucson.

Access: From Arizona State Highway 90 at a point 9 miles south of Benson (Interstate 10 Exit 302), and 10 miles north of the junction of Arizona State Highways 90 & 82 north of Sierra Vista, turn west into the park entrance.

Day Use Facilities: Large picnic area with shelters; group picnic areas with shelters; drinking water; restrooms; medium-sized parking lot.

Overnight Facilities: 62 campsites with electrical hookups; sites are small+, fairly level, with minimal separation; parking pads are medium-length straight-ins; water at several faucets; restrooms with showers; holding tank disposal statyion; oaved driveways; adequate to complete supplies

and services are available in Benson and Sierra Vista

Activities & Attractions: VGuided tours of the massive caverns (extra charge); 22,000-square-foot visitor center with informational displays and artifacts; including fiberglass replicas of cavern features.

Natural Features: Located on rolling, high-desert terrain at the foot of the Whetstone Mountains to the west; park vegetation consists of desert brush and succulents, dotted with hardwoods; park area is 550 acres; elevation 4600´.

Season & Fees: Open all year, except Christmas; reservation Fee: $3.00 (included in cave tour fee); Rotunda/Throne Room Tour: $9.95 (ages 7-13) and $18.95 (ages 14 & up), free for children 6 and younger; Big Room Tour: $12.95 (ages 7-13) and $22.95 (ages 14 & up), no children under 7; please see Appendix for standard Arizona state park entry and camping fees.

Mail & Phone: Kartchner Caverns State Park, P.O. Box 1849, Benson, Arizona 85602; tour reservations/park office ☎ (520) 586-CAVE (2283).

Park Notes: The existence of Kartchner Caverns was made public only in the late 1980's, even though they were discovered in the mid-1970's. Possibly the initial secrecy that had been maintained about the caverns and their whereabouts was meant to help safeguard them against vandalism. They contain over 2.5 miles of passages and at least two immense 'rooms'. One park information source claims that the caverns possess "world class features". They may be quite right.

* * * * *

Tonto Natural Bridge State Park, north of Payson, features North America's largest natural travertine bridge, and is located on land with some historical significance; limited facilities and access. Park office (928) 476-4202.

Notes & Sketches

New Mexico State Parks

Coronado State Park

 New Mexico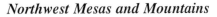

Northwest Mesas and Mountains

New Mexico 1 &

NAVAJO LAKE:
PINE RIVER
State Park

Location: Northwest New Mexico east of Farmington.

Access: From the junction of U.S. Highway 64 & New Mexico State Highway 539 (23 miles east of Bloomfield, 55 miles west of Dulce), travel north on Highway 539 for 5 miles, cross the dam, and continue for 0.5 mile beyond the dam to the park. **Alternate Access:** From the junction of U.S. 64 & New Mexico State Highway 511 (12 miles east of Bloomfield) head northeast on Highway 511 for 13.6 miles to the dam and continue as above.

Day Use Facilities: Medium-sized picnic area with several small ramadas (sun shelters); small group ramada; drinking water; restrooms; medium-sized parking area.

Overnight Facilities: 78 campsites, including 20 with electrical hookups or electrical and sewer hookups, in 5 loops; (additional sites are made available during peak periods); sites are generally small, with nominal separation; parking pads are mostly paved (some are gravel/dirt), short to medium straight-ins; most pads will require some additional leveling; small to medium-sized tent spots; a number of sites have ramadas (sun shelters); barbecue grills, plus some fireplaces; b-y-o firewood; water at central faucets; restrooms with showers; holding tank disposal station; most driveways are paved; gas and camper supplies at the marina; limited supplies and services are available in Bloomfield.

Activities & Attractions: Boating; boat launch; marina; fishing for rainbow trout, kokanee salmon, largemouth and smallmouth bass, northern pike, crappie, bluegill and catfish; well-equipped playground; small visitor center.

Natural Features: Located on a juniper-dotted sloping bluff at the southwest corner of 13,000-acre Navajo Lake, a reservoir on the San Juan River; junipers and pinon pines, on a surface of brush and sparse grass, provide minimal to light shade/shelter for picnic and camp sites; surrounded by mesas, with low mountains in the distance; total park land area is 18,000 acres (which includes property in all three developed recreation areas, plus a considerable amount of undeveloped/natural land); elevation 6100´.

Season & Fees: Open all year; please see Appendix for standard New Mexico state park entry and campground fees.

Mail & Phone: Navajo Lake State Park, 1448 NM 511 #1, Navajo Dam, NM 87419; ☎(505) 632-2278.

Park Notes: Lots of people come a long way to Navajo Lake—and they really can *see* a long way from here, too. Some sites along the rim of the bluff have superlative, 270° panoramas of the lake and the great expanse of this distinctive, red and green mesa country. Pine River is located near the confluence of the major secondary arm of the lake along the Pine River and the main body of the lake, which lies along the old San Juan River bed. From this elevated location you can look out onto several square miles of deep blue water. Navajo Lake backs up about 30 miles upstream of the dam all the way into Southern Colorado. (Pine River's Colorado cousin—Navajo Lake State Recreation Area near Arboles—is also an excellent facility.)

▲ **New Mexico 2**

NAVAJO LAKE:
SAN JUAN RIVER
State Park

Location: Northwest New Mexico east of Farmington.

Access: From the junction of U.S. Highway 64 & New Mexico State Highway 511 (12 miles east of Bloomfield) travel northeast on Highway 511 for 8 miles to the junction of Highway 511 and State Highway 173; turn northwest (left) onto Highway 173 and proceed (across the river) for 0.6 mile; turn northeast (right) onto a gravel/dirt local road (Simon Canyon Road) and drive 2.7 miles; then turn south (right) onto the Cottonwood area paved access road and proceed 1 mile to the park entrance; turn east (left) into the campground or continue ahead for a few yards to the day use area. (Note: signs indicate that Simon Canyon Road is "impassable when wet".)

Additional Access: From State Highway 511 near milepost 12 (by the Catholic church, 4 miles northeast of the junction of Highways 511 & 173), turn north onto a paved access road and proceed 0.25 mile to the San Juan Point day use area.

Day Use Facilities: Medium-sized picnic area, vault facilities and medium-sized parking lot at Cottonwood; medium-sized picnic area, vault facilities and medium-sized parking lot at San Juan Point.

Overnight Facilities: *Cottonwood Campground*: 47 campsites, including 2 handicapped-access units; sites are small to medium-sized, essentially level, with nominal separation; parking pads are paved, mostly medium+ to long straight-ins, plus a few pull-throughs; large areas for tents; fire rings; b-y-o firewood is recommended; water at several faucets; restrooms; holding tank disposal station; paved driveway; gas and camper supplies near Archuletta, 4 miles southwest; limited supplies and services are available in Bloomfield.

Activities & Attractions: Excellent fishing for trout on the river; paved trail from Cottonwood Campground to the riverbank; five handicapped-access fishing platforms and handicapped-access boat launch at the San Juan Point area; boating, boat launch, fishing for trout, kokanee salmon, bass, crappie, channel cat, etc. on Navajo Lake, 3 miles upstream.

Natural Features: Located on a large flat in a canyon along the north/west bank of the San Juan River below Navajo Dam; sites are very lightly to lightly shaded by hardwoods on a sandy/grassy surface; bordered by high, evergreen-dotted bluffs; elevation 5600´.

Season & Fees: Open all year; please see Appendix for standard New Mexico state park entry and campground fees.

Mail & Phone: Navajo Lake State Park, P.O. Box 6429, Navajo Dam, NM 87419; ☎(505) 632-1770.

Park Notes: One of the best stretches of trout water in the Southwest is along this riverbank. It wasn't always that way. Before Navajo Dam was finished in 1962, the San Juan was a swirling, muddy, silty stream during much of the year. Catfish were about the only game that could handle the murky water. Now the lake has a pronounced settling effect, and the broad San Juan runs clear and cold most of the time. Plenty of big browns, rainbows and cutthroats are here for the catching. The San Juan Point area is locally known as "Texas Hole" and all of you fishermen can probably figure out for yourselves how it got that handle.

▲ New Mexico 3

NAVAJO LAKE:
SIMS MESA
State Park

Location: Northwest New Mexico east of Farmington.

Access: From the junction of U.S. Highway 64 & New Mexico State Highway 527 (34 miles west of Dulce, 44 miles east of Bloomfield), journey northwest on Highway 527 for 17 paved miles to the park entrance; continue for 0.8 mile, (past the visitor center), then turn right into the main loop; or continue for an additional 0.1 mile and turn left into the upper loop.

Day Use Facilities: Medium-large picnic/camp area with shared facilities; several group ramadas (sun shelters).

Overnight Facilities: 43 camp/picnic sites in 2 loops; (additional, primitive sites are also available); sites are small to average in size, with nominal to fair separation; parking pads are short to medium-length, sand/earth straight-ins or pull-offs; many pads may require additional leveling; tent spots tend to be small, sloped and rocky; a number of sites have ramadas (sun shelters), b-y-o shade 'just in case'; fireplaces, plus some barbecue grills; b-y-o firewood; water at central faucets; restrooms; gas and camper supplies on Highway 64 about 20 miles south; limited supplies and services are available in Bloomfield and Dulce.

Activities & Attractions: Boating; boat launch; marina; fishing for rainbow trout, kokanee salmon, largemouth and smallmouth bass, northern pike, crappie, bluegill and catfish; small visitor center; hiking.

Natural Features: Located on a point on Sims Mesa at the southeast corner of Navajo Lake, a giant reservoir formed on the San Juan River; 13,000-acre Navajo Lake has 200 miles of shoreline; park vegetation consists of junipers, pinon pines, sagebrush, and sparse grass; most sites are on an open, lightly forested slope, a few sites are lakeside; many sites have good views through the trees of the lake and surrounding colorful mesas; the point is flanked by the main body of the lake to the north and the 4-mile-long Frances Creek arm of the lake to the south; Sims Mesa unit land area is 500 acres; elevation 6100´.

Season & Fees: Open all year; please see Appendix for standard New Mexico state park entry and campground fees.

Mail & Phone: Navajo Lake State Park, 1448 NM 511 #5, Navajo Dam, NM 87419; no telephone (mobile radio communications only).

Park Notes: It *is* possible to find seclusion at the end of a paved road. Sims Mesa tends to be much quieter than the other units on Navajo Lake. The unit here is seldom filled to capacity.

▲ New Mexico 4

HERON LAKE
State Park

Location: North-central New Mexico southwest of Chama.

Access: From U.S. Highway 84 near milepost 259 (2.2 miles north of Tierra Amarilla, 11 miles south of Chama), turn west onto New Mexico State Highway 95; travel southwest for 6.5 miles to the visitor center; or continue for another 0.3 mile, then turn northwest (right) for 0.2 mile then turn left into the Willow Creek Campground; or stay on the main road for another 1.5 miles to the Brushy Point area; or continue beyond the Brushy Point turnoff for an additional mile to the Island View area; or a final mile past Island View and across the dam to the Ridge Rock area.

Day Use Facilities: Small to medium-sized picnic/camp areas with vault facilities and small parking areas at Brushy Point and Island View.

Overnight Facilities: *Willow Creek Campground*: 22 campsites, including 8 with partial hookups; sites are medium-sized or better, with pretty fair separation; parking pads are gravel, medium to long straight-ins or pull-throughs; many pads may require a little additional leveling; adequate space for at least a medium-sized tent in most units; barbecue grills; b-y-o firewood is recommended; water at faucets; restrooms; holding tank disposal station; gravel driveways; additional camp/picnic sites are available at Brushy Point and Island View; gas and camper supplies 3 miles east on Highway 95, gas and groceries in Tierra Amarilla.

Activities & Attractions: Fishing for rainbow trout and kokanee salmon; limited boating (trolling speed max); sailing; boat launch; nature trail in the Willow Creek area; visitor center with interpretive displays; Rio Chama hiking trail from Heron Lake to its neighbor to the southwest, El Vado Lake.

Natural Features: Located on forested hills overlooking 5900-acre Heron Lake; a great 'notch' or gap can be seen across the lake where 2 mesas meet; park vegetation consists of tall ponderosa pines, fairly dense junipers, pinon pines, sage, and grass; some lake views through the trees; park land area is 4100 acres; elevation 7200´.

Season & Fees: Open all year; please see Appendix for standard New Mexico state park entry and campground fees.

Mail & Phone: Heron Lake State Park, P.O. Box 31, Rutheron, NM 87563; ☎(505) 588-7470.

Park Notes: Heron Lake offers some *really* pretty scenery. The lake has been designated as a "quiet lake" and is geared especially toward activities such as fishing, sailing, canoeing and hiking. Although Willow Creek provides the best value for the camping dollar, the views are better at Brushy Point and Island View. Heron Lake is connected by trail to El Vado Lake and the route is a popular one with families or groups with differing recreational preferences: part of the party can travel between the lakes via the fairly easy trail while the others go around by motorized land locomotion. Heron Lake State Park is also connected historically with Green River State Park in Utah. The Dominguez-Escalante expedition passed through here, as it did through Green River, on its famous exploratory trip through the Southwest in 1776.

▲ New Mexico 5

EL VADO LAKE
State Park

Location: North-central New Mexico southwest of Chama.

Access: From U.S. Highway 84 near milepost 258 (1.3 miles north of Tierra Amarilla, 12 miles south of Chama), turn west onto New Mexico State Highway 112; head southwest for 12.1 miles to near milepost 33; turn north onto a gravel/dirt access road and continue for 4.5 miles to the park.

Day Use Facilities: Large picnic/camp area with shared facilities; group ramadas.

Overnight Facilities: Approximately 50 camp/picnic sites in 3 loops; sites are small to medium-sized, with minimal to fair separation; parking surfaces are level, gravel/earth/grass, medium to long straight-ins or pull-offs; most sites have large, level, grassy tent spots; a number of sites have ramadas (sun shelters); fireplaces; b-y-o firewood is recommended; water at several faucets; restrooms, plus auxiliary vaults; gravel driveways; gas and groceries in Tierra Amarilla.

Activities & Attractions: Boating; boat launch; (another boat launch is located at the north end of El Vado Lake and is accessible from off of State Highway 95 west of Heron Lake State Park); fishing for rainbow and brown trout and kokanee salmon; ice fishing and cross-country skiing; Rio Chama Trail, an excellent 5.5-mile-long hiking and ski trail, connects El Vado Lake with Heron Lake, northeast of here; Rio Chama Wildlife Area is adjacent to the park.

Natural Features: Located on a grassy bluff above El Vado Lake, a 3500-acre reservoir formed on Rio Chama; Loops A and B are situated right along the edge of the bluff overlooking the lake; Loop C is tucked away along a tiny bay 0.2 mile behind the main camp/picnic area; a few conifers are scattered around the windswept, sage-dotted bluff; the lake and basin are surrounded by pine-and-juniper-covered hills, mountains and mesas; park land area is 1728 acres; elevation 6900´.

Season & Fees: Open all year, with limited services November to April; please see Appendix for standard New Mexico state park entry and campground fees.

Mail & Phone: El Vado Lake State Park, P.O. Box 29, Tierra Amarilla, NM 87575; ☎(505) 588-7247.

Park Notes: If you want to get away from it all, this could be the place. 'Though the access is a trifle rough at times, and the facilities a bit basic, you do have some outstanding views of the wide open spaces. It might be really difficult to decide which is the more comely of the two sisters: El Vado Lake or nearby Heron Lake. Solution: spend equal time with both of them.

▲ **New Mexico 6**

FENTON LAKE
State Park

Location: North-central New Mexico north of Albuquerque.

Access: From the junction of New Mexico State Highways 4 and 126 (9 miles north of Jemez Springs, 30 miles west of Los Alamos), proceed 9.3 miles west (the last mile is gravel) past the lake on the left; turn south (left) into Fenton Lake State Park; proceed 0.6 mile (past the boat ramp and park office) to the campground. (Fenton Lake State Park is also accessible from the west, from Cuba, but a portion of the 33 miles of road from Cuba to Fenton Lake has a dirt/gravel surface and is impassable in inclement weather).

Day Use Facilities: Picnic/camp area with shared facilities; group picnic area (available by reservation only); additional day use area on the northeast shore of the lake.

Overnight Facilities: 30 camp/picnic sites, including 2 handicapped-access units; most sites are large and well separated; parking pads are gravel/dirt, short to medium-length straight-ins; many pads will require additional leveling; a few large level, grassy tent spots near the creek, but most tent areas are rather sloped; fireplaces; gathering

firewood on national forest land along the way to the park, or b-y-o, is recommended; water at a central faucet near the boat ramp; vault facilities; gravel/dirt driveways; gas and groceries 9 miles east.

Activities & Attractions: Fishing for stocked rainbow and brown trout; handicapped-access fishing pier; limited boating (people-power only, no motors or sails); boat launch; 5-mile hiking/cross-country ski trail; biathlon rifle range; state fish hatchery, 4 miles west.

Natural Features: Located on the west shore of Fenton Lake, a 30-acre recreational impoundment on Rio Cebolla, and along the west bank of the river below the dam; sites stretch for over a mile along the lake and river, a few are along a creek; some sites are in tall grass and others are situated in an open conifer forest; a number of small side streams enter the lake and river in this area; the lake is bordered by marsh areas, and the forested slopes and rocky palisades of the Jemez Mountains; park land area is 290 acres; elevation 7700´.

Season & Fees: Open all year, with limited services November to April; please see Appendix for standard New Mexico state park entry and campground fees.

Mail & Phone: Fenton Lake State Park, P.O. Box 555, Jemez Springs, NM 87025; ☎(505) 829-3630.

Park Notes: The drive up to Fenton Lake is quite an experience—this timbered mountain country is impressive. Facilities in the park may not be the Southwest's best, but the scenery, seclusion, and opportunities for placid recreation and contemplation are very good.

▲ **New Mexico 7** ♿

BLUEWATER LAKE
State Park

Location: Northwest New Mexico northwest of Grants.

Access: From Interstate 40 Exit 63 for Prewitt (37 miles west of Grants, 43 miles east of Gallup), turn south onto New Mexico State Highway 412 and travel 6 miles to the park. (Note: most maps show a paved road from the nearby town of Thoreau to the lake, but the park isn't accesible via that route.)

Day Use Facilities: Several medium to large camp/picnic areas with shared facilities; group picnic area.

Overnight Facilities: Approximately 50 camp/picnic sites, including some with electrical hookups; (a number of primitive camp spots are also available); sites are small to medium-sized, with relatively little separation; most parking pads are gravel, a few are paved; most pads are short to medium-length straight-ins, a few are long pull-throughs; additional leveling will probably be required in most sites; tent areas tend to be small and sloped; some sites have framed-and-gravelled table/tent areas; fireplaces; b-y-o firewood is suggested; water at several faucets; restrooms with showers; holding tank disposal station; paved/gravel driveways; gas and camper supplies at small local stores; adequate supplies and services are available in Grants.

Activities & Attractions: Boating; boating launch and dock; fishing (reportedly quite good) for stocked rainbow trout; small playground.

Natural Features: Located on fairly steep, rolling slopes around the north-east end of 2300-acre Bluewater Lake, in a large basin encircled by low hills; park vegetation consists mostly of pinon pines and junipers which provide limited shelter/shade, plus very sparse grass; the roughly 'T'-shaped lake (on the national forest map it resembles one of those high-tech golf putters) impounds Bluewater Creek to the south and Cottonwood Creek to the west; the Continental Divide lies along the Zuni Mountains to the south and west; typically breezy; park land area is 2200 acres; elevation 7400´.

Season & Fees: Open all year, subject to winter weather and road conditions, with limited services November to April; please see Appendix for standard New Mexico state park entry and campground fees.

Mail & Phone: Bluewater Lake State Park, P.O. Box 3419, Prewitt, NM 87045; ☎(505) 876-2391.

Park Notes: There's a continuous climb on Highway 412 from the Interstate to the lake. As you drive along, you'll probably experience noticeable temperature changes, even though the elevation difference between the freeway and the lake is only about 600´. Camp/picnic sites have creek canyon views or lake views, depending upon the particular section in which they are situated. (Subjectively, the sites in the Creek Overlook section, though smallish and close together, are some of the more attractive ones in the park.) Bluewater is said to be one of the most popular trout fishing lakes in New Mexico. From certain areas within the park there are some very impressive views of 11,000´ Mount Taylor in the distant east.

🔺 **New Mexico 8** ♿

CORONADO
State Park

Location: Central New Mexico north of Albuquerque.

Access: From Interstate 25 at Bernalillo Exit 242 (21 miles north of Albuquerque, 43 miles south of Santa Fe), travel west on New Mexico State Highway 44 for 1.7 miles (to a point 0.25 mile west of the Rio Grande bridge; turn north (right) onto a paved access road, proceed 0.15 mile, then turn east (right again), into the park; continue east directly into the campground, or turn north (left) and proceed 0.3 mile on the park driveway to the picnic area. (Note: if northbound, signs may advise you to take Exit 240 to the park; that's OK, if you want the grand tour of Bernalillo; for a direct route, take Exit 242 directly onto Highway 44.)

Day Use Facilities: Medium-sized picnic area; several ramadas; drinking water; restrooms; medium-sized parking lot.

Overnight Facilities: 23 campsites, including 15 with partial hookups; (several primitive/undeveloped sites are also available); sites are small to medium-sized, with nominal separation; parking pads are paved, mostly level, long pull-throughs; small, fairly level, tent areas; adobe ramadas (sun/wind shelters) for all developed units; barbecue grills; b-y-o firewood; water at faucets throughout; restrooms with showers; paved driveways; limited+ supplies and services are available in Bernalillo.

Activities & Attractions: Coronado State Monument (a unit of the Museum of New Mexico, adjacent to the state park) has a visitor center with exhibits about the prehistory and history of the Rio Grande Valley, and an interpretive trail through partially reconstructed ruins of Kuaua Pueblo; limited boating/canoeing and fishing on the river; playground.

Natural Features: Located on the west bank of the Rio Grande; park vegetation consists of tall grass and a few hardwoods and small conifers; surrounded by the semi-arid plain of the Rio Grande Valley; the Sandia Mountains rise to the east; park area is 218 acres; elevation 5000´.

Season & Fees: Open all year; please see Appendix for standard New Mexico state park entry and campground fees.

Mail & Phone: Coronado State Park, P.O. Box 853, Bernalillo, NM 87004; ☎(575) 867-5589.

Park Notes: It had been a long and tough 18 months when Francisco Vasquez de Coronado arrived here on the banks of the Rio Grande and decided to spend the winter of 1540-1541. Coronado had come from Mexico with a ragtag caravan of about 300 troops, 800 Indians, and a take-along, fast food menu of chickens, pigs and cattle. The Southwest's first European explorer had come here searching for the fabled Cities of Gold. What he found was a centuries-old Indian village earning a marginal subsistence by farming, foraging and hunting. In the spring of 1541, after a bitter winter spent bickering with the local Indians over what few rations there were to share between them, the expedition pushed on toward the north then east. Coronado went as far as the Oklahoma Panhandle and Southwest Kansas before giving up the quest for gold and returning to Mexico in 1542. No gold in New Mexico? Just set up a picnic or camp site, light a fire, and then watch the evening sun cast shadows on the Sandias and reflections on the Rio Grande.

▲ New Mexico 9 ⅙

RIO GRANDE NATURE CENTER
State Park

Location: Central New Mexico in Albuquerque.

Access: From Interstate 40 Exit 157 for Rio Grande Boulevard on the northwest quadrant of Albuquerque (3 miles west of the junction of Interstate Highways 40 & 15 near midtown, 1 mile east of the Rio Grande bridge), proceed north on Rio Grande Boulevard for 1.4 miles; turn west (left) onto Candelaria Road NW and continue for 0.7 mile to the park parking lot; the visitor center is 0.2 mile north, via a wide foot trail. (Note: Turnaround space at the end of the dead-end street is somewhat limited, but there's even less in the parking lot.)

Day Use Facilities: Drinking water and restrooms inside the visitor center; medium-sized parking lot; additional, streetside parking is available just outside the park.

Overnight Facilities: None; nearest public campground is in Coronado State Park.

Activities & Attractions: Visitor center with interpretive displays about the natural history and ecology of the Rio Grande Valley, small classroom and laboratory, library; self-guided nature trails; guided nature walks; bike trail; small, outdoor amphitheater; (guide pamplets are available).

Natural Features: Located in a woodland (*bosque*) along the east bank of the Rio Grande in the North Valley area; park vegetation consists of large cottonwoods and other hardwoods, brush, and tall grass; the Sandia Mountains rise a few miles east; park area is 170 acres; elevation 5000´.

Season & Fees: Open all year, except for a few major holidays (hours vary, and are subject to change); park entry fee $1.00 for children, $2.00 for adults.

43

Mail & Phone: Rio Grande Nature Center, 2901 NW Candelaria Road, Albuquerque, NM 87107; ☎(575) 344-7240.

Park Notes: First stop here should be the visitor center. The main passageway leading into the building is a sewer pipe. (Well, OK, actually, it's a section of corrugated steel culvert about 8 feet in diameter.) Once inside, the first items you'll probably notice are more than a dozen transparent plastic columns, each about a foot-and-a-half in diameter, which reach from floor to ceiling. Modern Art? No, they're designed to demonstrate one of the methods of using solar energy. Each of the columns is filled with about 100 gallons of water. They're designed to gather the sun's energy from the building's skylights, diffuse the light throughout the central room, and store the heat inside the column. In practice, the installation here involves some limiting factors, so the efficiency of the system is about 20 percent—but the idea certainly is worth demonstrating. Albuquerque is noted for its pioneering advances in the use of sun power, and an appropriate place for a demonstration of same is a nature education center. The columns also visually enhance the scientific atmosphere, and in fact provide an almost futuristic, science fiction-like ambience.

One of the major attractions of the park is the 'duck pond', which is designed to replicate a so-called "Oxbow" lake. (Before the Rio Grande was 'tamed' by dams, the river would create horseshoe-shaped lakes as it changed course during its flood-and-ebb cycles. The only other state park on the Rio Grande with an oxbow lake is Bentsen-Rio Grande State Park in South Texas.) There are three ways to view the pond: in the outdoors, through one of the 'sidewalk superintendent' peepholes cut into a wooden retaining wall along a trail; indoors, through a wall of picture windows from a seat in a special viewing room; or through a 'submarine' window which is like an upside-down periscope that gives you a glimpse of pond life *below* the surface. As you peer into *your* side of the window, try to imagine what *you* look like to the fish, frogs, turtles, and diving ducks who are looking into *their* side of the window!

 New Mexico

Northeast Mountains & High Plains

▲ New Mexico 10

SUGARITE CANYON
State Park

Location: Northeast New Mexico northeast of Raton.

Access: From Interstate 25 Exit 452 in Raton, travel east/northeast on New Mexico State Highway 72 for 3.7 miles to a fork in the road; take the left fork (actually almost straight ahead) onto State Highway 526; continue northerly for 1.4 miles to the park entrance; proceed 1.6 miles to the Lake Alice area; or continue for another 1.1 miles, then turn west (left) onto the Soda Pocket Campground access road (gravel) and climb 1.6 miles up a steep and twisty road to the campground; or go north past the Soda Pocket turnoff for an additional 1.7 miles to the Lake Maloya area.

Day Use Facilities: A couple-dozen picnic sites along the east and southwest shores of Lake Maloya; medium-sized picnic area just north of Lake Alice; drinking water; vault facilities; small parking area; also, group picnic/camp area (reservations required) at Soda Pocket.

Overnight Facilities: *Soda Pocket Campground*: 34 campsites, including 6 walk-in units; (a group camp/picnic area is also available, by reservation); sites are medium to large, with nominal to fairly good separation; parking pads are gravel, medium to medium+ straight-ins; some pads will require additional leveling; some very nice tent areas; fire rings; b-y-o firewood is recommended; water at a central pipe; vault facilities; gravel driveway; a few additional walk-in camp/picnic sites are available at Lake Alice; complete supplies and services are available in Raton.

Activities & Attractions: Visitor center; exhibits including remnants of buildings from a formerly thriving coal-mining town; fishing for stocked rainbow trout; handicapped-access fishing pier at the north end of Lake Maloya; limited boating (no gas motors) and boat launch on Lake Maloya, very limited boating on tiny Lake Alice; nature trail; hiking trails in the mountains and around the lakes; cross-country skiing.

Natural Features: Located in a forested canyon in the high foothills east of the Rockies; day use areas and lakes are on the canyon floor; Soda Pocket is in a mountain meadow with minimal shade/shelter, bordered by a fairly dense forest of pines, junipers and hardwoods; a striking rimrock formation towers over the campsites; 3 small lakes are in the canyon—Alice and Maloya in New Mexico, and Dorothy, just across the border in Colorado; a small stream flows between the lakes; 85 acres of water and 3600 acres of land are within the park; elev. 7800´.

Season & Fees: Day use areas open all year; Soda Pocket Campground open May to October; please see Appendix for reservation information and standard New Mexico state park entry and campground fees.

Mail & Phone: Sugarite Canyon State Park, HCR 62, BOX 386, Raton, NM 87740; ☎ (505) 445-5607.

Park Notes: Sugarite formerly was the site of a booming coal camp of the early 1900's, with a population that fluxed between 400 and 1000 souls. Many of the miners were immigrants from the Old Country—Czechs, Irish, Italians, Japanese and Slavs. The visitor center has a collection of old photos and other memorabilia from that bygone era. Since it's also a state highway, the park road is a surprisingly busy thoroughfare all year long. Spring through fall, vacationers use it as a fine reason to take a break from the Interstate, and locals use the slow-paced scenic drive as a good excuse to get out of town. In winter, the locals come out on sunny Sundays and skiers use it to reach the Sugarite ski area north of the border. One of the park's special places is Soda Pocket. The area high above the canyon floor is unseen by most visitors. There are some terrific views down the canyon and out onto the plains from up there. (Incidentaly, the name of the park is pronounced like *sugar-eat´*.)

▲New Mexico 11

CIMARRON CANYON:
PALISADES & TOLBY
State Park

Location: Northern New Mexico between Taos and Raton.

Access: From U.S. Highway 64 at milepost 288 +.8 (4 miles east of Eagle Nest, 20 miles west of Cimarron), turn north into *Tolby* campground; or at milepost 294, turn south into *Palisades* picnic area. (Special Note: The west park boundary is near milepost 288 +.5; the east park bounbdary is near milepost 295 +.7.)

Day Use Facilities: Small picnic area; vault facilities; medium-sized parking lot; also, there are several small or medium-sized parking lots located a few yards off the highway along the 7-mile canyon drive; many small roadside pullouts are also along the route.)

Overnight Facilities: 24 campsites; sites are generally small, level, and rather closely spaced; parking pads are paved, short to medium-length straight-ins; mostly small, grassy tent spots; barbecue grills; a very limited amount of firewood is available for gathering in the area, so b-y-o is recommended; water at several faucets; vault facilities; paved driveways; gas and groceries+ are available in Eagle Nest and Cimarron.

Activities & Attractions: Trout fishing; extensive backcountry hiking; 8-mile drive through highly scenic Cimarron Canyon; picturesque Eagle Nest Lake, 5 miles west, is a privately owned lake where boating is permitted for an additional charge.

Natural Features: Located along the Cimarron River in Cimarron Canyon; picnic sites are moderately shaded; almost half the campsites are riverside; campground vegetation consists of tall hardwoods, junipers, grass and an assortment of other smaller hardwoods and brush; Cimarron Canyon is renowned for its impressive steep canyon walls of crenellated granite; elevation 8000´.

Season & Fees: Open all year, with limited services October to April; 14 day camping limit; please see Appendix for standard New Mexico state park fees.

Mail & Phone: Cimarron Canyon State Park, P.O. Box 147, Ute Park NM 87749; ☎ (505) 377-6271.

Camp Notes: There's a superb trip through Cimarron Canyon to Tolby, which is only one of four camp areas in Cimarron Canyon State Park. Each of the campground environments varies a bit, so if you have the time, it might be worth a few minutes to take a look at all four--Tolby, Blackjack, Maverick and Ponderosa. This segment of the Cimarron River is renowned for its fine trout fishing. (Special 'regs' apply.)

🌲**New Mexico 12**

CIMARRON CANYON:
BLACKJACK
State Park

Location: Northern New Mexico between Taos and Raton.

Access: From U.S. Highway 64 at milepost 292 +.6 (7 miles east of Eagle Nest, 23 miles west of Cimarron), turn south into the campground parking lot; campsites are located along a foot trail within 100 yards of the west end of the lot.

Day Use Facilities: Most facilities are shared with campers (daylight hours only).

Facilities: 5 walk-in tent campsites; sites are small+, reasonably level, with fairly good separation; adequate space for medium to large tents; no drinking water in the campground; drinking water is available at Tolby and Maverick Campgrounds (see separate information); vault facilities; paved parking lot (for vehicles of tent campers only after dark, no rv's); gas and groceries+ are available in Eagle Nest and Cimarron.

Activities & Attractions: Scenic, 7-mile drive through Cimarron Canyon; fishing for trout in the Cimarron River (said to be very good); fishing in Gravel Pit Lakes near Maverick Campground (see info); extensive backcountry hiking; U.S. 64 follows the Mountain Branch of the historic Santa Fe Trail.

Natural Features: Located on a small, gently rolling flat along the Cimarron River in Cimarron Canyon in the Cimarron Range of the Sangre de Cristo Mountains; sites are shaded/sheltered mostly by medium-dense, tall conifers; elevation 8000´.

Season & Fees: Open all year, with limited services October to April; please see Appendix for standard New Mexico state park fees.

Mail & Phone: Cimarron Canyon State Park, P.O. Box 147, Ute Park NM 87749; ☎ (505) 377-6271.

Park Notes: One of the park's most notable features, the 'Palisades' rise from the canyon floor just opposite the Blackjack area. The barren-faced cliffs aren't plainly visible from the campsites, but a two-minute walk across the highway will bring you to their base.

🌲**New Mexico 13** ♿

CIMARRON CANYON:
MAVERICK
State Park

Location: Northern New Mexico between Taos and Raton.

Access: From U.S. Highway 64 at milepost 295 +.3 (10 miles east of Eagle Nest, 13 miles west of Cimarron), turn north into the campground.

Day Use Facilities: Medium-sized parking area; other facilities are shared with campers.

Overnight Facilities: 48 campsites in 2 loops; sites are small, essentially level, with minimal to nominal separation; parking pads are paved, short straight-ins; enough room for small to medium-sized tents; barbecue grills; b-y-o firewood is recommended; water at central faucets; restrooms, plus auxiliary vaults; paved driveways; disposal station across the highway at Ponderosa Campground; paved driveways; gas and groceries in Eagle Nest.

Activities & Attractions: Stream fishing for trout; fishing (but no swimming, wading or rock plopping) in Gravel Pit Lakes; backcountry hiking in the state wildlife preserve; 8 mile scenic drive through Cimarron Canyon.

Natural Features: Located along the Cimarron River in Cimarron Canyon; Gravel Pit Lakes are within a stone's throw of many of the sites; (Gravel Pit Lakes... stone's throw... get it? Ugh. Ed.); vegetation consists of tall conifers, a few junipers, a little underbrush, and grass; this section of Cimarron Canyon has steep canyon walls of intense shades of gold and orange; elevation 8000´.

Season & Fees: Open all year, with limited services October to April; 14 day camping limit; please see Appendix for standard New Mexico state park fees.

Mail & Phone: Cimarron Canyon State Park, P.O. Box 147, Ute Park NM 87749; ☎ (505) 377-6271.

Park Notes: Just across the highway and two-tenths of a mile to the east is the park's Ponderosa Campground. The camping arrangement there consists of a large paved lot with medium to long pull-off parking spaces for 14 vehicles. The campground's fireplaces, central water and holding tank disposal station are separated from the highway by a stand of conifers.

🌲 **New Mexico 14** ♿

COYOTE CREEK
State Park

Location: North-central New Mexico north of Las Vegas.

Access: From New Mexico State Highway 434 at milepost 17 (3 miles north of Guadalupita, 17 miles north of Mora, 19 miles south of Angel Fire), turn east/southeast onto the park access road and proceed 0.1 mile; turn left to the hookup area, or right to the standard campsites.

Day Use Facilities: Large picnic/camp area with shared facilities; small group shelter.

Overnight Facilities: 26 camp/picnic sites, including a half-dozen with partial hookups; sites vary from small and very closely spaced in the hookup zone to very large and very well spaced in the standard area; parking pads are gravel, mostly medium to long straight-ins or pull-offs; hookup pads are basically level, others will require some additional leveling; adequate, though generally sloped, space for large tents in most sites; a dozen standard sites have Adirondack shelters (a log structure with three-sides and a slanted roof); fire rings; b-y-o firewood is recommended; water at several faucets; vault facilities; holding tank disposal station; rocky gravel driveways; park host; nearest supplies and services (limited) are in Mora.

Activities & Attractions: Fishing (stream is stocked regularly with trout); hiking trail (starts at the east end of the park, crosses a creek bridge, traverses the side of the mountain, and then comes back down into the valley and across another creek bridge); playground.

Natural Features: Located along Coyote Creek in a valley in the Sangre de Cristo Mountains; hookup sites are on an open flat; standard sites are in a brush-lined meadow along the creek or on adjacent hillsides; hillside sites are sheltered by large oaks and some tall conifers; several beaver ponds on the creek; bordered by forested mountains; elevation 8000´.

Season & Fees: Open all year, with limited facilities in winter; please see Appendix for standard New Mexico state park entry and campground fees.

Mail & Phone: Coyote Creek State Park, P.O. Box 291, Guadalupita, NM 87722; ☎ (505) 387-2328.

Park Notes: You shouldn't feel lacking in elbow room here. The relatively few camp/picnic sites are spread out over about a half square mile of lush, green countryside.

🌲 **New Mexico 15**

MORPHY LAKE
State Park

Location: North-central New Mexico north of Las Vegas.

Access: From New Mexico State Highway 94 at milepost 14 + .4 (on the north edge of the hamlet of Ledoux, 4 miles south of Mora, 27 miles north of Las Vegas) turn northwest and make your way up a steep, winding dirt road for 3 miles to the park. (Note: signs indicate "Not recommended for camper trailers", see Park Notes, below.)

Day Use Facilities: Medium-sized camp/picnic area with shared facilities.

Overnight Facilities: Approximately 12 primitive camp/picnic sites in an open camping arrangement; ample space for any size vehicle you can haul up here; tables and fire facilities for most sites; some firewood is available for gathering in the surrounding area; no drinking water; vault facilities; dirt driveway; gas and snacks in Ledoux; limited supplies and services are available in Mora.

Activities & Attractions: Fishing for regularly stocked trout; limited boating/canoeing (hand-propped or electric motors); small boat launch.

Natural Features: Located on a grassy flat along the north-east shore of 25-acre Morphy Lake; the lake lies in a conifer-coated basin on the east slope of the Sangre de Cristo Mountains; park land area is 240 acres; elevation 7800´.

Season & Fees: Available all year, subject to weather conditions; principal season is June through September; please see Appendix for standard New Mexico state park entry and campground fees.

Mail & Phone: c/o Coyote Creek State Park P.O. Box 291, Guadalupita, NM 87722; ☎(505) 387-2328.

Park Notes: Most of the dirt track into Morphy Lake also serves as a logging road, so if you decide to give it a try, keep in mind that the log trucks know the road better than you do. A 4wd vehicle is recommended, and even then it might be a bit of a drill getting up and down in inclement weather. The park is a designated primitive-use area. If you do make the trip to the lake, it will be a rewarding experience—this is a gem in the rough.

▲ **New Mexico 16** ♿

STORRIE LAKE
State Park

Location: North-central New Mexico north of Las Vegas.

Access: From New Mexico State Highway 518 at a point 4.6 miles north of downtown Las Vegas, 8 miles south of Sapello), turn west into the park. (Quickest access from Interstate 25, northbound or southbound, is to take Exit 347 at the north end of Las Vegas, then south on Grand Avenue for 1.3 miles to Mills Avenue, west on Mills for 0.8 mile to Highway 518/7th Street, then north on Highway 518 for 3.6 miles to the park; if you're northbound, this adds a couple of miles vs the through-town business route from Exit 343, but the bypass will save time and stop-and-go fuel—especially if you lose your way winding through downtown.)

Day Use Facilities: Medium-sized picnic/camp area with shared facilities; small group shelter.

Overnight Facilities: 25 camp/picnic sites, including 10 with partial hookups; sites are medium to large, with fair to good separation; parking surfaces are gravel, level, long straight-ins and pull-offs; large, mostly level, tent spots; barbecue grills plus a few fireplaces; b-y-o firewood; water at several faucets; restrooms with showers; paved main driveway; complete supplies and services are available in Las Vegas.

Activities & Attractions: Boating; windsurfing; boat launch and dock; fishing; beach access; playground; ball field; exercixe trail; small visitor center.

Natural Features: Located in a wide valley along the southeast shore of 1100-acre Storrie Lake; the lofty, forested peaks of the Sangre de Cristo Mountains rise to the west; park vegetation consists of a few planted hardwoods, scattered junipers, and bunchgrass; typically breezy; park land area is 82 acres; elevation 6400´.

Season & Fees: Open all year, with limited services November to April; please see Appendix for standard New Mexico state park entry and campground fees.

Mail & Phone: Storrie Lake State Park, P.O. Box 3157, Las Vegas, NM 87701; ☎(505) 425-7278.

Park Notes: Storrie Lake is perfect for anyone who enjoys wide open spaces close to town. From everywhere in the park there's a super view of the lake, and across the wide valley to picturesque, high, timbered mountains. Lots of elbow room here. (If you're just passing by, the entire park is in full view from the highway.) Besides super scenery, some significant state history is associated with this area: Las Vegas was a major stop on the Santa Fe Trail; it was here that General Stephen Kearney announced the annexation of New Mexico by the U.S in 1846; and the town served as a territorial capitol-in-exile during the occupation of Santa Fe by Confederate forces during the War Between the States. (Somehow it just doesn't seem possible for that conflict to have ever reached this far West.) One more thing: this Las Vegas is the *original* Las Vegas.

▲ **New Mexico 17**

SANTA FE RIVER
State Park

Location: North-central New Mexico in Santa Fe.

Access: From the intersection of U.S. Highways 84/285 (Saint Francis Drive) and Cerrillos Road near midtown Santa Fe (3.2 miles north of Interstate 25 Exit 282), turn northeast onto Cerrillos Road and proceed 0.9 mile; turn east onto Alameda Street and go through downtown for 0.2 mile to the park, along the south (right) side of Alameda. (Notes: Santa Fe traces its lineage back about 400 years, so it isn't at all like one of those new 'planned' cities with dull streets all neatly lined up north-south or east-west; there are a dozen ways of getting downtown from various places around the city; but using the major intersection at Saint Francis Drive and Cerrillos Road as a reference gives you a relatively easily found point from which to begin your local quest.)

Day Use Facilities: Several picnic tables and small benches situated along the riverbank; limited streetside parking.

Overnight Facilities: None; nearest public campground is in Hyde Memorial State Park.

Activities & Attractions: Cultural and historical significance.

Natural Features: Located along the banks of the Santa Fe River; vegetation consists mainly of sections of mown grass, rows of large hardwoods, and shrubs; park area is 5 acres; elevation 7000´.

Season & Fees: Open all year; (no fee).

Mail & Phone: c/o New Mexico State Parks Headquarters, 408 Galisteo, Santa Fe NM 87504; ☎(575) 827-7465.

Park Notes: The park boundary isn't closely defined, but it more or less starts just west of the corner of East Alameda and Old Santa Fe Trail (near the Supreme Court building) and extends approximately a half mile eastward. From the state park limit are similar Santa Fe city parks which stretch westward for several tenths of a mile along the river. Both areas serve well as downtown coffee-lunch-shopping break spots. This heart-of-the-city section along the river is called "The Alameda". Check your Spanish-English dictionary, (if you already know both languages you're excused), and you'll see that *alameda* can mean a "mall", "grove", or "shaded walk". In this case, all three English equivalents are meaningful. The park itself is just a narrow strip of land along a riverbed and, depending upon the climatic cycle and the season, the stream may or may not be flowing when you stroll along its shaded banks. This small, simple state park and its city park sisters in themselves wouldn't merit a special side trip if you're just going by on the Interstate or on your way up North through town. But without them Santa Fe probably wouldn't be Santa Fe.

▲ New Mexico 18

HYDE MEMORIAL
State Park

Location: North-central New Mexico east of Santa Fe.

Access: From the intersection of U.S. Highways 84/285 (Saint Francis Drive) and Paseo de Peralta near midtown Santa Fe (4 miles north of Interstate 25 Exit 282), proceed east on Paseo de Peralta for 1 mile to Washington Drive; turn north (left) for 0.2 mile to Artist Drive; turn east (right) and continue on Artist Drive, which becomes Hyde Park Road (State Highway 475), for 7.6 miles northeast to the park boundary; picnic and camp sites stretch for a mile along both sides of the road; hookup camp sites are at the far north end of the park.

Day Use Facilities: Very large picnic/camp area with shared facilities; group shelters (available by reservation).

Overnight Facilities: 84 camp/picnic sites, including 7 with electrical hookups; sites are medium to large with fair to good separation; most parking pads are gravel/dirt, short to medium straight-ins or pull-offs; hookup site pads are paved straight-ins; many pads may require additional leveling; tent spots may be a bit sloped; 42 units have Adirondack shelters (lean-to log structures with 3 sides, a slanted roof and a chimneyed fireplace); fireplaces or fire rings in most sites, barbecue grills in the hookup units; some firewood is usually available for gathering in the surrounding national forest, b-y-o to be sure; water at central faucets; vault facilities; holding tank disposal station; gravel/dirt driveways; complete supplies and services are available in Santa Fe.

Activities & Attractions: Hiking on 5 trails, including access to the Pecos Wilderness; playgrounds; cross-country skiing; sledding; ice skating pond.

Natural Features: Located on forested slopes in the Sangre de Cristo Mountains; Little Tesuque Creek flows within a few yards of many sites; park vegetation consists of tall ponderosa pines, other conifers, a few aspens, light underbrush and grass; park area is 350 acres; elevation 8300´ to 8600´.

Season & Fees: Open all year, with limited services November to April; please see Appendix for standard New Mexico state park entry and campground fees.

Mail & Phone: Hyde Memorial State Park, P.O. Box 1147, Santa Fe, NM 87504; ☎(575) 983-7175.

Park Notes: Hyde Park is especially popular with forest hikers. The high altitude and steep trails offer an invigorating workout. The mountainsides along the highway are just covered with picnic and camp sites. The unusual (for this part of the country anyway) Adirondack shelters here are similar to those in a number of other parks and national forest camps in New Mexico. They appear to have been built by the Civilian Conservation Corps. Likewise, the ornate and practical rockwork around some of the sites displays the influence, if not the actual handiwork, of CCC craftsmen. Only ten minutes out of downtown, Hyde Park is, as one park worker put it "one of the best-kept secrets in Santa Fe".

▲ New Mexico 19 ♿

VILLANUEVA
State Park

Location: North-central New Mexico southwest of Las Vegas.

Access: From New Mexico State Highway 3 at milepost 60 +.7 at the northern edge of the community of Villanueva (11.5 miles south of the junction of State Highway 3 & Interstate 25, 20.5 miles north of the junction of State Highway 3 & Interstate 40), turn southeast onto a paved park access road; continue easterly for 1.5 miles to the park entrance; most camp/picnic sites are located in clusters flanking the paved main park road over the next half mile, (turnaround loop at the end); a group of sites is on a short hill above the main road. (Note: Highway 3 is tolerable from Interstate 40; on the road map it looks deceptively straight along the Pecos River from I-25; it is, in reality, very twisty and slow-going.)

Day Use Facilities: Large picnic/camp area with shared facilities; group ramada.

Overnight Facilities: 23 developed camp/picnic sites; (a number of undeveloped/primitive camp/picnic sites are also available); sites are medium or better in size, and fairly well separated; parking pads are gravel/dirt, short to medium-length straight-ins or pull-offs; parking pads in the upper section may require additional leveling; some nice, large tent spots along the river, but those up on the hillside are smaller and sloped; a few sites have adobe ramadas (sun/wind shelters); barbecue grills; b-y-o firewood; water at several faucets; restrooms with showers; paved or dirt/gravel driveways; gas and groceries in Villanueva.

Activities & Attractions: Fishing for rainbow trout; foot trails with historical markers; (Coronado may have passed through here in 1541; by the late 1500's, this became a segment of the 'Route of the Conquistadores'); playground; footbridge over the river; small visitor center.

Natural Features: Located in a canyon (or a narrow valley) along the winding Pecos River; bordered by vertical red sandstone canyon walls to the east, tree-dotted hills to the west; park vegetation consists of canyon live oak, juniper, cholla and prickly pear cactus, and sparse grass; the vast Glorieta Mesa rises a few miles northwest of here; park area is 1000 acres; elevation 5600´.

Season & Fees: Open all year; please see Appendix for standard New Mexico state park entry and campground fees.

Mail & Phone: Villanueva State Park, General Delivery, Villanueva, NM 87583; ☎(505) 421-2957.

Park Notes: The larger recreation sites are in a really terrific riverside location, and the sites perched up on the hillside offer an excellent vantage point. Visitor's choice in this department. The natural setting is inviting: it's in a boundary zone between the mountains and the plains.

▲ **New Mexico 20**

CLAYTON LAKE
State Park

Location: Northeast corner of New Mexico northwest of Clayton.

Access: From U.S. Highways 64 & 87 on the north/west edge of Clayton, turn north onto New Mexico State Highway 370 and travel on a generally northwesterly course for 10.5 miles; turn west (left) onto State Highway 455 for 1.5 miles to the park entrance; picnic and camp sites are located in a number of clusters around the south and west sides of the lake.

Day Use Facilities: Large picnic/camp area with shared facilities; small group ramada.

Overnight Facilities: 40 camp/picnic sites; (several primitive sites are also available); sites are medium to large, with fairly good to very good separation; parking pads are gravel, short to medium-length straight-ins or pull-offs; some pads will require additional leveling; medium to large, generally sloped and somewhat rocky, tent spots; ramadas (sun shelters) for a number of sites; barbecue grills; b-y-o firewood; water at central faucets; restrooms with showers, plus auxiliary vaults; main driveway is paved part-way, gravel sub-drives; adequate supplies and services are available in Clayton.

Activities & Attractions: Fishing for stocked bass, catfish, and rainbows; limited boating; boat launch and dock; dinosaur tracks exhibit (at the northeast end of the lake, acessible via a foot trail which crosses the dam; playground.

Natural Features: Located on a bluff and its lower slope around the south and west shores of Clayton Lake, a 176-acre impoundment on Seneca Creek; park vegetation consists mostly of junipers and sparse, tall grass; surrounding countryside is primarily hilly grassland, and a few low mountains; park land area is 417 acres; elevation 5200´.

Season & Fees: Open all year, with limited services October to March; please see Appendix for standard New Mexico state park entry and campground fees.

Mail & Phone: Clayton Lake State Park, Star Route, Seneca, NM 88437; ☎(505) 374-8808.

Park Notes: Although the elevation here is only about mile-high, the surrounding open countryside has the appearance of being twice that. The alpine illusion adds an intriguing element to this buffer zone between the High Plains and the Rockies. If you'd like to take a short stroll a long way back into time, a nature trail will lead you to a group of several hundred dinosaur footprints. It seems a family of five dinos wandered through here about a 100 million years ago and their passage through what then was a mud flat is now registered in hardened rock.

🌲 New Mexico 21 ♿

CHICOSA LAKE
State Park

Location: Northeast New Mexico northeast of Las Vegas.

Access: From New Mexico State Highway 120 at milepost 81 +.7 (7 miles north of Roy, 36 miles southwest of the junction of State Highway 120 and U.S Highway 56 southwest of Clayton), turn north onto a gravel local road and proceed 0.8 mile; turn west (left) onto the state park access road and continue for 0.4 mile to the campground.

Day Use Facilities: Large camp/picnic area with shared facilities.

Overnight Facilities: 12 standard campsites (a number of primitive/very basic camp/picnic sites around the lake shore are also available); sites are medium-sized, with nominal separation; parking surfaces are gravel, medium to long, straight-ins/pull-offs; some additional leveling (or maneuvering) will probably be required in most sites; large, slightly sloped tent areas; ramadas (adobe sun/wind shelters) for standard campsites; barbecue grills; b-y-o firewood; water at faucets throughout the principal camping area; restrooms with showers, plus auxiliary vault facilities;

limited supplies and services are available in Roy.

Activities & Attractions: Historical and informational exhibits, including an old-fashioned chuck wagon; small herd of longhorn cattle; fishing for stocked rainbow trout; limited boating; playground.

Natural Features: Located on grassy, treeless slopes above the south and east shores of 40-acre Chicosa Lake, a small, natural lake surrounded by gently rolling prairie; Kiowa National Grassland lies north and west of the park; forested mountains are visible in the distant north and west; park land area is 600 acres; elevation 6000´.

Season & Fees: Open all year (principal season is April to November), with limited services in winter; please see Appendix for standard New Mexico state park entry and campground fees.

Mail & Phone: Chicosa Lake State Park, General Delivery, Roy, NM 87743; ☎(505) 485-2424.

Park Notes: Chicosa Lake served as a watering stop for cattle drives on the famous Goodnight-Loving Trail, a major route from Texas to Wyoming during the late 1860's and early 1870's. The trail was named for Charles Goodnight and Oliver Loving, pacesetters in the cattle business who blazed the trail in 1866. Their aim was to get their stock to the first northern markets to open up for longhorn cattle following the War Between the States. Because thousands of Texas farmers and ranchers had left their homes to fight for the Confederacy, scores of thousands of longhorns had gone wild during their five-year absence.

After the war, at least a million longhorns needed to be rounded up and taken to ready markets in the East and North. More than a quarter-million cattle were driven along the 2000-mile-long Goodnight-Loving Trail from Fort Belknap to Cheyenne during the nine years the trail was actively used. The park's purpose, therefore, is historical as much as it is recreational. The isolation and vastness which you can see and sense here is probably very close to what you might have experienced as a trail boss or a drover on the way north to Cheyenne. (If you've ever seen the old Clint Eastwood TV series

Rawhide—which some pundits dubbed "History's Longest Cattle Drive"—you'll really appreciate Chicosa Lake.)

▲ New Mexico 22

UTE LAKE:
NORTH
State Park

Location: Eastern New Mexico northeast of Tucumcari.

Access: From U.S. Highway 54 at milepost 326 in midtown Logan (24 miles northeast of Tucumcari, 27 miles southwest of the New Mexico-Texas border), turn west onto New Mexico State Highway 540; proceed 2.4 miles, then turn south (left, at the park office), and continue for 0.1 mile to the camp/picnic area.

Day Use Facilities: Medium-sized picnic and camp area just south of the main campground and along the lake shore; a few sites have small ramadas (sun shelters).

Overnight Facilities: 24 campsites with partial hookups; (a number of standard/semi-primitive camp/picnic sites are also available); sites are average-sized, essentially level, with minimal separation; parking pads are paved, medium-length pull-throughs or short to medium-length, wide straight-ins; adequate space for a large tent in most sites; barbecue grills; b-y-o firewood; water at faucets throughout; restrooms; holding tank disposal station near the park office; paved driveways; limited supplies and services are available in Logan.

Activities & Attractions: Fishing for walleye, crappie, white and largemouth bass, channel catfish; boating; boat launches, marina nearby; small ball fields; designated orv (off road vehicle) areas, about 4 miles north.

Natural Features: Located on a slightly sloping flat near the north shore of the main part of Ute Lake; vegetation consists of short grass, and planted hardwoods that provide minimal to nominal shade/shelter in most hookup sites; other picnic/camp sites receive little or no shade; surrounded by dry plains, hills and bluffs; typically breezy; total park land area is 1500 acres; elevation 3800´.

Season & Fees: Open all year (principal season is April to November); please see Appendix for standard New Mexico state park entry and campground fees.

Mail & Phone: Ute Lake State Park, P.O. Box 52, Logan, NM 88426; ☎ (505) 487-2284.

Park Notes: Just across the lake from the North area is the contrasting South area. From U.S. 54 near milepost 324 (2 miles south of Logan), drive a mile west to what is essentially an undeveloped/primitive section of the park. Another site on the south shore is the primitive campground at Mine Canyon. To get there, find milepost 317 +.2 on U.S. 54, (9 miles south of Logan) then go north on a local access road for a mile. The lake's surrounding countryside is interesting in its own rough-hewn fashion. Ute Lake reportedly provides the best walleye fishing in New Mexico. If you don't fish, but have a boat, you can explore the dozens of coves and small side canyons around the lake.

▲ New Mexico 23 ♿

UTE LAKE:
LOGAN
State Park

Location: Eastern New Mexico northeast of Tucumcari.

Access: From U.S. Highway 54 at milepost 326 in the town of Logan (24 miles northeast of Tucumcari, 27 miles southwest of the New Mexico-Texas border), turn west onto New Mexico State Highway 540; proceed 4.9 miles (the road curves sharply around to the north at 4.5 miles); turn west (left) into the campground.

Day Use Facilities: Medium-sized picnic/camp area with vault facilities just west of the main camping area; picnic/camp sites also in the nearby Windy Point and Rogers areas.

Overnight Facilities: 24 campsites with partial hookups; (a number of standard/semi-primitive camp/picnic sites with small ramadas are also available); sites are medium-sized, level, with nominal separation; parking pads are paved, medium-length pull-throughs or short to medium-length, wide straight-ins; large tent areas; barbecue grills; b-y-o firewood; water at faucets throughout; restrooms with showers; holding tank disposal station; paved driveways; limited supplies and services are available in Logan.

Activities & Attractions: Fishing for walleye, white and largemouth bass, crappie, channel catfish; boating; boat launches; marina; Cedar Valley Nature Trail; designated orv (off road vehicle) areas, in the Rogers neighborhood, about a mile northwest.

Natural Features: Located on a bluff above a bay on the east shore of the Ute Creek arm of Ute Lake, an 8000-acre reservoir on the Canadian River; (the Ute Creek arm is a major tributary extending northward from the main body of the basically east-west lake); local vegetation consists of short grass, plus small hardwoods and a few evergreens that provide minimal shade/shelter in some sites; several small, rocky islands dot the lake surface; surrounded by dry plains, and evergreen-dotted hills and bluffs; typically breezy; total park land area is 1500 acres; elevation 3800´.

Season & Fees: Open all year (principal season is April to November); please see Appendix for standard New Mexico state park entry and campground fees.

Mail & Phone: Ute Lake State Park, P.O. Box 52, Logan, NM 88426; ☎(505) 487-2284.

Park Notes: Of the several camping areas on Ute Lake, Logan quite possibly offers the best combination of facilities, attractiveness, and views. If you're camping and don't need a hookup, you might want to consider the camp/picnic sites just west of the hookup district. They're located on several small, unsheltered points, they're generally well-spaced, most have ramadas, and the views are unrestricted. Two other small picnic/camp areas adjacent to Logan—Windy Point 0.2 mile south, and Rogers 1

mile north/northwest—each offer similar standard sites and surroundings.

▲ New Mexico 24 ♿

CONCHAS LAKE
State Park

Location: Eastern New Mexico northwest of Tucumcari.

Access: From New Mexico State Highway 104 at milepost 75 + .6 (31 miles northwest of Tucumcari, 75 miles southeast of Las Vegas), turn north onto a paved access road and proceed 0.2 mile; turn west (left, just past the information station) onto a paved road and continue for 0.75 mile, then turn north (right) for 0.1 mile to the South unit of the park. **Alternate Access:** From Interstate 40 Exit 300 for Newkirk, (26 miles northeast of Santa Rosa, 33 miles southwest of Tucumcari), travel north on State Highway 129 for 17.2 miles to its junction with State Highway 104; bear northeasterly (right) onto Highway 104 and proceed 6 miles to the park turnoff at milepost 75 + .6 and continue as above.

Day Use Facilities: Large camp/picnic area with shared facilities.

Overnight Facilities: 65 camp/picnic sites, including several with partial hookups; sites are medium to large, with reasonable to fairly good separation; parking pads are gravel/earth, medium to long straight-ins or pull-offs; a little additional leveling may be required in many sites; adequate space for a medium to large tent in most units; many sites have ramadas (sun or sun/wind shelters); assorted fire appliances; water at faucets throughout; restrooms; holding tank disposal station; gravel or paved driveways; camper supplies at the marina; adequate supplies and services are available in Tucumcari.

Activities & Attractions: Boating; boat launch; marina; fishing for largemouth and smallmouth bass, channel cat, crappie, bluegill and walleye; children's playground; 9-hole golf course (adults' playground); 4800´ paved and lighted airstrip (on the south side of Highway 104; you'll have to hoof it for a few hundred yards to the first tee if you fly in with your foursome for a day on the links).

Natural Features: Located on a slope near the south shore of Conchas Lake, a 25-mile-long, 9000-acre reservoir at the confluence of the Conchas and Canadian Rivers; most sites are very lightly to lightly shaded/sheltered by medium-large hardwoods and some junipers on a surface of tall grass; grassy plains, plus some colorful, juniper-dotted hills and escarpments, surround the area; total park land area is 1160 acres; elevation 4200´.

Season & Fees: Open all year (principal season is April to November) with limited services in winter; please see Appendix for standard New Mexico state park entry and campground fees.

Mail & Phone: Conchas Lake State Park, P.O. Box 976, Conchas Dam, NM 88416; ☎(505) 868-2270.

Park Notes: Conchas Lake is unusual in that, although it impounds two rivers, the main body of water lies over the old Conchas Riverbed, rather than along the region's major stream, the Canadian River. The Conchas arm of the lake averages about a mile in width; the long, serpentine Canadian arm is a third of that span. The facilities described here are in the park's 'South' area along the south shore of the main body of the lake; the park's 'North' area, 4 miles north of this unit along the Canadian River, has leased, concession-operated facilities. *Conchas* means 'shells' and perhaps the name refers to some sort of freshwater mollusks found in the old riverbed.

▲ **New Mexico 25** ♿

SANTA ROSA LAKE
State Park

Location: Eastern New Mexico north of Santa Rosa.

Access: From Interstate 40 (eastbound) Exit 273 for Santa Rosa, travel east on Business Route I-40 for 1 mile into midtown Santa Rosa to the intersection of Parker Avenue & Second Street; turn north (left) onto North Second Street and proceed north

on North Second, east (right) on Eddy Avenue, then north on Eighth Street (you'll pass under the Interstate) and continue northerly on a paved road for 7 miles to the park boundary; continue northwest for 0.5 mile to a point just before the dam, then turn northeast (right) for 0.2 mile to the Juniper picnic area and boat launch; or continue across the dam and north for an additional 1.5 miles to Rocky Point Campground.

Alternate Access: From Interstate 40, (westbound) Exit 275, travel west on Business I-40 for 1.1 mile into midtown Santa Rosa to Parker & Second and continue as above. (Note: Once you get into midtown Santa Rosa you should be able to pick up signs directing you along the above route; if all the signs are in place, you can just use these instructions as a series of checkpoints.)

Day Use Facilities: Medium-sized picnic area; ramadas (sun shelters) for all sites; drinking water; restrooms; parking area.

Overnight Facilities: *Rocky Point Campground*: 50 campsites, including many with electrical hookups; (a primitive camp area near the Juniper picnic area is also available); sites are medium to medium+, with fair to good separation; parking pads are paved, medium to long pull-throughs or medium-length straight-ins; additional leveling probably will be required in most sites; ramadas (sun/partial wind shelters) for nearly all sites; medium to large areas for tents; barbecue grills; b-y-o firewood; water at several faucets; restrooms with showers; holding tank disposal station near the park entrance; paved driveways; adequate supplies and services are available in Santa Rosa.

Activities & Attractions: Boating; boat launch; fishing for walleye, bass and catfish; a scenic trail (0.4 mile) at the southeast end of the dam, a handicapped-access scenic/nature trail at the northwest end of the dam (0.75 mile), and a small visitor center are on Corps of Engineers turf, adjacent to the park.

Natural Features: Located on a hillside above the west shore of Santa Rosa Lake, a 2400-acre reservoir on the Pecos River;

park vegetation consists of scattered, large and small junipers, some low-level brush, cactus and short grass; surrounded by rolling plains, bluffs, distant hills and mesas; elevation 4800´.

Season & Fees: Open all year, with limited facilities in winter; please see Appendix for standard New Mexico state park entry and campground fees.

Mail & Phone: Santa Rosa Lake State Park, P.O. Box 384, Santa Roas, NM 88435; ☎(505) 472-3110.

Park Notes: The 'mechanical' description of the park and its near and far surroundings really doesn't do justice to this excellent spot. The countryside around here has what could be described as a 'fresh, clean look'. Subjectively, the park has one of the nicer state park campgrounds in New Mexico, or anywhere in the High Plains for that matter. (Santa Rosa Lake and its recreation facilities were initially developed by the Corps of Engineers. A unique feature of the project is the CoE handicapped-access loop trail, with viewpoints of the Pecos River and its attendant canyon downstream of the lake.) From virtually anywhere in the state park, the panoramas are simple, but vast.

 New Mexico ⚑
Southwest High Desert

🔺 **New Mexico 26**

SENATOR WILLIE M. CHAVEZ
State Park

Location: Central New Mexico south of Albuquerque.

Access: From Interstate 25 Exit 190 (northbound), travel north into midtown Belen on Business Route I-25 (Main Street) for 2.1 miles to the corner of Main Street & Reinken Avenue; turn east (right) onto Reinken Avenue/New Mexico State Highway 309 and proceed east on Highway 309 for 2.1 miles; turn south (right) into the camping area; or continue east for another 0.1 mile, then turn south into the picnic area. **Alternate Access:** From Interstate 25 Exit 196 (southbound), head south into midtown Belen on Business Route I-25 for

4.1 miles to the corner of Main and Reinken; turn east (left) onto Highway 309 and continue as above. (Note: Most maps depict Highway 309 only as an unnumbered, short, east-west route that connects downtown Belen with State Highway 47 east of Belen; the park is just 0.2 mile west of the junction of Highways 47 & 309.)

Day Use Facilities: Medium-sized picnic area; group picnic area; drinking water, restrooms medium-sized parking lot adjacent to the campground; random parking in the picnic area.

Overnight Facilities: 10 campsites, including 6 with partial hookups; sites are small, level, with minimal to nominal separation; parking pads are gravel, mostly long pull-throughs; tent space varies from very small to large; small ramada (sun shelter); fire rings; b-y-o firewood; water at sites and at central faucets; restrooms; mostly gravel driveways; virtually complete supplies and services are available in Belen.

Activities & Attractions: Nature trail; fishing for stocked trout in the "ditch" that flows between the picnic and camp area; playground.

Natural Features: Located on grassy flats along or near the west bank of the Rio Grande; picnic sites are along the riverbank and receive light to medium shade from large hardwoods; campsites are on a flat above the river and are minimally to lightly shaded; a large, mown lawn and a landscaped garden area are adjacent to the campground; the Manzano Mountains rise above 10,000´ to the east; park area is 107 acres; elevation 4800´.

Season & Fees: Open all year; please see Appendix for standard New Mexico state park entry and campground fees.

Mail & Phone: Senator Willie M. Chavez State Park, 1617 East River Road, Belen, NM 87002; ☎(505) 864-3915.

Park Notes: Looking for something to do while you're picnicking or camping here? Try for the trout in the "ditch". Trout are regularly stocked in the swiftly flowing water, which is thought to originate mostly from underground springs. This nice little park, formerly called Belen Valley State Park, was renamed for the late United States Senator Willie Chavez, who was from Belen.

▲ New Mexico 27

MANZANO MOUNTAINS
State Park

Location: Central New Mexico southeast of Albuquerque.

Access: From New Mexico State Highway 55 at milepost 76 +.7 near the south end of the small community of Manzano (24 miles north of Mountainair, 31 miles south of Interstate 40 Exit 175 east of Albuquerque), turn southwest (i.e., bear right if southbound, sharp left if northbound) onto a paved local road and continue for 0.1 mile, then turn right and travel 3.3 miles on another paved road, which becomes gravel, to the park.

Day Use Facilities: Small picnic area; group ramada.

Overnight Facilities: 17 campsites, including 6 with electrical hookups; sites are fairly large and well separated; parking pads are gravel, reasonably level, medium to long straight-ins; medium-sized tent areas; ramadas (sun/wind shelters) for a few sites; handicapped unit; barbecue grills; firewood is usually for sale, some firewood may be available for gathering on adjacent national forest land, b-y-o to be sure; water at several faucets; restrooms; holding tank disposal station; gravel driveway; camper supplies in Manzano; limited supplies and services are available in Mountainair.

Activities & Attractions: Several miles of hiking trails in the area; nature trail, (easy walking, 0.5 mile loop); playground; game court; possibilities for x-c skiing on trails and unplowed back roads; Quarai Ruins unit of Salinas National Monument, 1 mile southwest of the nearby hamlet of Punta de Aqua (via a paved road).

Natural Features: Located on the lower slopes of the Manzano Mountains; park vegetation consists mostly of moderately dense, medium-height pines; 10,100´ Manzano Peak rises among the well-forested mountains to the west; the vast plains of eastern New Mexico lie to the east; occasional heavy snowfall; park area is 160 acres; elevation 7200´.

Season & Fees: Open all year (subject to brief closures due to winter weather conditions); please see Appendix for standard New Mexico state park entry and campground fees.

Mail & Phone: Manzano Mountains State Park, Route 2 Box 52, Mountainair, NM 87036; ☎ (505) 847-2820.

Park Notes: Manzano Mountains is one of those neat, little, sequestered parks that doesn't get a lot of notoriety because anyone who's been here dummies-up about the place and keeps it for themselves. If you're looking for a simple hideaway with pleasant mountain and valley views, and yet is less than ninety minutes' drive from the state's largest city, this could be the spot you seek.

▲ New Mexico 28 ♿

ELEPHANT BUTTE LAKE
State Park

Location: Southwest New Mexico northeast of Truth or Consequences.

Access: From Interstate 25 (southbound), Exit 83 (6 miles north of Truth or Consequences), pick up New Mexico State Highway 195 on the east side of the Interstate; head southeast on Highway 195 for 4.1 miles; turn northerly (left) into the park entrance; continue ahead for 0.7 mile to the standard sites along the edge of the bluff (on the east side of the main road); or turn west into the large, hookup camp area on the hillside; or continue past the hookup zone to the primitive sites scattered along the shore.

Alternate Access: From Interstate 25 (northbound), take Exit 79 (1 mile north of T or C), and proceed to the east side of I-25; travel east and northeast on a well-signed route along New Mexico State Highways 181 and 171 for 3.7 miles; turn southeast onto State Highway 195 for a final 0.8 mile to the park entrance turnoff, and continue as above. (Notes: State Highways 171, and 181 are short connecting roads which aren't shown on most maps; also, approach the primitive sites in sandy areas along the shore with a measure of skepticism—and a winch.)

Day Use Facilities: Several large areas with picnic/camp sites along a 2-mile stretch of lake shore; large group shelter (available by reservation); drinking water; restrooms; parking at sites.

Overnight Facilities: 111 campsites with electrical or partial hookups (dozens of standard and primitive camp/picnic sites are also available); sites in the hookup section are medium-sized, with nominal separation; most parking pads are paved, and vary from medium-length straight-ins to very long pull-throughs; most pads will require additional leveling; (certain sites in the hookup section are available by reservation only, contact the park office); standard camp/picnic sites are fairly large and well spaced, with reasonably level, gravel parking pads; adequate room for a small tent in most sites; many sites have ramadas (sun or sun/wind shelters); barbecue grills; b-y-o firewood; water at hookups and at central faucets; restrooms with showers; holding tank disposal station; paved driveways; camper supplies at nearby stores; adequate supplies and services are available in Truth or Consequences.

Activities & Attractions: Fishing for bass, channel catfish and crappie; boating; boat launch; large playground; small visitor center with interpretive displays related to the natural, historical and cultural facets of the region; designated orv area.

Natural Features: Located above the west shore of Elephant Butte Lake, an irrigation reservoir on the Rio Grande; (typical surface area is about 18,000 acres, maximum surface area is about twice that number); hookup sites are on a slope, remaining sites are on a short bluff above the lake shore or along a sandy beach; vegetation consists primarily of desert brush, plus a few hardwoods and a couple of junipers; low bluffs flank the lake, lofty mountains are visible in the distance; total park land area is 20,500 acres (although only a portion of its acreage has been developed); elevation 4400´.

Season & Fees: Open all year; please see Appendix for standard New Mexico state park entry and campground fees.

Mail & Phone: Elephant Butte Lake State Park, P.O. Box 13, Elephant Butte, NM 87935; ☎(505) 744-5421.

Park Notes: Named after a local landmass that fancifully resembles the head of a gentle pachyderm rising from the water, Elephant Butte Lake is the largest reservoir in New Mexico. (Although it has since been eclipsed by other projects, Elephant Butte was, upon its completion in 1916, the largest man-made reservoir in the world.) Fishing is productive year 'round, and the lake hosts quite a few bass tournaments. As for picnicking and camping: there are many first-rate sites in both the standard and hookup neighborhoods; almost all sites have good views, and some vistas are really panoramic.

Finally, just in case you haven't heard the story of how Truth or Consequences acquired its unique moniker: As part of a 1950 promotional campaign, broadcasting's Ralph ("This is Your Life") Edwards promised fame to any town which would rename itself after his top-rated radio show, "Truth or Consequences". The citizens of what was formerly named Hot Springs, New Mexico saw the move as a great way to generate some national publicity for their town (let alone some much-needed income), and jumped at the opportunity to hitch their municipal wagon to a star. The rest, as they say, is history.

▲ **New Mexico 29** ♿

CABALLO LAKE:
LAKESIDE
State Park

Location: Southwest New Mexico south of Truth or Consequences.

Access: From Interstate 25 Exit 59 (20 miles south of Truth or Consequences, 52 miles northwest of Las Cruces), from the east side of the Interstate, travel northeast on New Mexico State Highway 187 for 1 mile, then turn right, to the park entrance station; curve north (left) and continue for 0.1 mile to the camping/picnicking sections.

Day Use Facilities: Very large camp/picnic area; drinking water; central restrooms.

Overnight Facilities: 44 camp/picnic sites, including 34 with partial hookups, in basically 3 sections; (primitive, 'open' camping/picnicking is also available in large areas north and south of Lakeside, and also on the lake's southeast shore, at the east end of the dam); sites in the hookup sections are in gravel, semi-parking lot arrangements, with medium to long, straight-in or pull-along parking spaces; not much tent space; sites have small ramadas (sun shelters) over table areas; the 10 sites in the third section are spacious, with fairly good separation, and have good-sized, gravel parking areas, and large, adobe ramadas (sun/wind shelters); barbecue grills; b-y-o firewood; water at several faucets; restrooms with showers; holding tank disposal station; camper supplies just outside the park on Highway 187; adequate supplies and services are available in T or C.

Activities & Attractions: Boating; boat launch with large parking lot; marina; fishing for bass, catfish, panfish; hiking trails; playground.

Natural Features: Located on a bluff above Caballo Lake, a 15-mile-long, 11,000-acre reservoir on the Rio Grande; park vegetation consists mostly of desert brush, plus some planted prickly pear, ocotillo, and yucca; the barren-looking Caballo Mountains rise sharply from the east shore of the lake; typically breezy; total park area is 5300 acres; elevation 4200´.

Season & Fees: Open all year; please see Appendix for standard New Mexico state park entry and campground fees.

Mail & Phone: Caballo Lake State Park, P.O. Box 32, Caballo, NM 87931; ☎(505) 743-3942.

Park Notes: The park's various picnic/camp districts are appropriately named for *caballos*: Appaloosa, Palomino, Arabian, Thoroughbred—so pick the breed of steed that suits you. The individual units with the adobe ramadas are extra nice.

They're not only larger and better spaced, but some are situated along the edge of the bluff, so the lake views are a little better than from many of the other sites. (But watch that lonnnnng step if you wander around after dark. Splash!) The lake takes its name from the Caballos Mountains (*Sierra de los Caballos*, or *Sierra Caballo*), which had been named for the herds of wild horses that roamed there. Local legend has it that the horses were descendants of those ridden into New Mexico by Coronado and the members of his expedition in 1540.

▲ **New Mexico 30**

CABALLO LAKE:
RIVERSIDE
State Park

Location: Southwest New Mexico south of Truth or Consequences.

Access: From Interstate 25 Exit 59 (20 miles south of Truth or Consequences, 52 miles northwest of Las Cruces), proceed northeast on New Mexico State Highway 187; after 100 yards, turn east (right) onto a paved access road that leads toward the dam; continue for 0.3 mile, then bear right just on the west side of the dam and continue for a final 0.75 mile down into the park.

Day Use Facilities: Medium-sized camp/picnic area; drinking water; central restrooms; parking in, or adjacent to, sites.

Overnight Facilities: 45 camp/picnic sites; sites are medium-sized, level, with minimal to fair separation; most parking pads are gravel/earth straight-ins or pull-offs; drivewayside parking is available for some sites; excellent tent-pitching possibilities; fireplaces, fire rings, and/or barbecue grills; b-y-o firewood; water at several faucets; restrooms; holding tank disposal station, 2 miles north in the park's Lakeside section; camper supplies, 2 miles north on Highway 187; adequate supplies and services are available in Truth or Consequences.

Activities & Attractions: Boating, boat launch, and fishing for bass, catfish, panfish on Caballo Lake; playground.

Natural Features: Located on a flat along the Rio Grande just below Caballo Lake Dam; sites are sheltered/shaded by medium to tall hardwoods on a grassy surface; dry bluffs and the Caballo Mountains are somewhat visible to the south and east; elevation 4200´.

Season & Fees: Open all year; please see Appendix for standard New Mexico state park entry and campground fees.

Mail & Phone: Caballo Lake State Park, P.O. Box 32, Caballo, NM 87931; ☎(505) 743-3942.

Park Notes: If you don't require an unrestricted view, such as those in the park's other area (Lakeside), this might be your spot. In fact, when the wind picks up (as it does on a daily basis around here), this might be *the* spot to be.

▲ New Mexico 31 ♿

PERCHA DAM
State Park

Location: Southwest New Mexico south of Truth or Consequences.

Access: From Interstate 25 Exit 59 for Caballo and Percha Dam State Parks (20 miles south of Truth or Consequences, 52 miles northwest of Las Cruces), travel south/southwest on New Mexico State Highway 187 for 1 mile; turn east (left) onto a gravel/dirt access road and proceed east and south for 1.2 miles to the park.

Day Use Facilities: Medium-sized camp/picnic area with shared facilities; central adobe ramada (sun/wind shelter) suitable for small groups; parking at sites and in open areas.

Overnight Facilities: Approximately 30 camp/picnic sites, including 6 with partial hookups; sites are small to medium-sized, basically level, with minimal to nominal separation; parking surfaces are gravel/earth, short straight-ins or long pull-throughs; adequate space for medium to large tents; ramadas (sun shelters) for about a dozen sites; barbecue grills; b-y-o firewood is recommended; water at hookups and at central faucets; restrooms with showers; gravel/earth driveway; camper supplies on Highway 187, 1 mile northeast of the freeway exit.

Activities & Attractions: Short hiking trails along the river; fishing (primarily catfish); birding; playground; Percha Dam, a historic, small diversion dam built to redirect water for irrigation purposes as part of the Rio Grande project of the early 1900's.

Natural Features: Located along the west bank of the Rio Grande in the Rio Grande Valley; sites receive light to medium shade/shelter from large cottonwoods and other hardwoods, plus some pines and junipers/cedars; large, open, grassy area adjacent to the camp/picnic sites; river views from some sites; bordered by a plain and by dry, rocky hills and mountains; park area is 84 acres; elevation 4200´.

Season & Fees: Open all year; please see Appendix for standard New Mexico state park entry and campground fees.

Mail & Phone: c/o Caballo Lake State Park, P.O. Box 32, Caballo, NM 87931; ☎(505) 743-3942.

Park Notes: Unless the highway maintenance folks have run a blade over the access road just before your arrival (or the road has been recently black-topped), you'll need a max-clearance vehicle with beefy tires to make it through deep, hardened ruts or gumbo-slick mud (depending upon the weather). If you're looking for a little more seclusion than might be available elsewhere around here (and you're sure you can make it in and out), then this park might be worth a look. There's plenty of shade, grass, and room. The mature vegetation here is part of the natural *bosque* ('woodland') which originally cloaked the banks of the Rio Grande.

▲ New Mexico 32 ♿

LEASBURG DAM
State Park

Location: South-central New Mexico north of Las Cruces.

Access: From Interstate 25 Exit 19 for Radium Springs (15 miles north of Las Cruces, 22 miles south of Hatch), turn west and proceed 0.8 mile on a paved local road; turn north (right) onto a dirt/gravel access road and continue for 0.3 mile to the park entrance station; 0.1 mile beyond the entrance turn left into the hookup area; or continue straight ahead for another 0.4 mile to the remaining camp/picnic section.

Day Use Facilities: Medium-large picnic/camp area with shared facilities.

Overnight Facilities: Approximately 25 camp/picnic sites, including several with partial hookups; (primitive campsites in an area along the river below the main park are also available); sites are average-sized, level, with minimal to nominal separation; parking pads are gravel, mostly short to medium-length straight-ins, plus a few pull-throughs; adequate space for a tent (may be best on the parking surface, if you have a free-standing tent); adobe ramadas (sun/wind shelters) for most sites; barbecue grills; b-y-o firewood; water at several faucets; restrooms with showers; holding tank disposal station; gravel driveways; complete supplies and services are available in Las Cruces.

Activities & Attractions: Limited boating/canoeing and fishing; unique playground, constructed mostly of adobe.

Natural Features: Located on a desert plain in the Mesilla Valley above the Rio Grande; vegetation consists almost exclusively of desert brush; low hills and barren mountains lie in the surrounding area; park area is 140 acres; elevation 4200´.

Season & Fees: Open all year; please see Appendix for standard New Mexico state park entry and campground fees.

Mail & Phone: Leasburg Dam State Park, P.O. Box 61, Radium Springs, NM 88054; ☎(505) 524-4068.

Park Notes: During much of the year, the Rio Grande is only a trickle as it passes by here, so fishing and boating aren't prime attractions. This is mostly just a fairly good, convenient, high desert campground that's reportedly very popular in winter or just about any time the local college is in session.

▲ **New Mexico 33** ♿

CITY OF ROCKS
State Park

Location: Southwest New Mexico northwest of Deming

Access: From New Mexico State Highway 61 at milepost 3 +.2 (3.2 miles northeast of the junction of State Highway 61 and U.S. Highway 180 between Deming and Silver City, 22 miles southeast of the junction of State Highways 61 & 152 near San Lorenzo), turn north onto a paved park access road and proceed 1.5 miles to the park entrance, then a final 0.3 mile on gravel to the camp/picnic areas.

Day Use Facilities: Very large camp/picnic area with shared facilities.

Overnight Facilities: 56 camp/picnic sites in a central city and a suburb; most sites are large to very large, with ample to excellent separation; majority of the parking pads are gravel straight-ins of various lengths, many are long pull-throughs; most pads will require at least a little additional leveling; tent areas vary from small to large, and may be slightly sloped; some sites have stone-framed table/fire pads; fireplaces or fire rings; b-y-o firewood; water at central faucets; vault facilities in the camp/picnic ground, restrooms near the park office; gravel driveways; adequate to complete supplies and services are available in Deming or Silver City.

Activities & Attractions: Trail through desert botanical gardens; playground; small visitor center.

Natural Features: Located around the base of a large cluster of huge, eroded, volcanic rocks standing on end; park vegetation consists of sparse grass, desert plants, junipers and oaks; nominal shelter/shade is provided by trees or large rocks in almost every site; surrounded by vast expanses of desert plains and dry mountains; park area is 680 acres; elevation 5200´.

Season & Fees: Open all year; please see Appendix for standard New Mexico state park entry and campground fees.

Mail & Phone: City of Rocks State Park, P.O. Box 50, Faywood, NM 88034; ☎ (505) 536-2800.

Park Notes: If you're a resident of a modern city or a bedroom community you'll probably appreciate the layout here. The camp/picnic units aren't laid out in 'tract' formation like those in so many other parks; instead, they're fairly widely spaced in natural coves, nooks and cubbies among the rocks. A number of them are in cul-de-sacs situated off of the main parkway. By stopping for a day or staying for a night and rubbing elbows with these smoothly eroded volcanic giants you probably can gain a greater appreciation for this unique natural feature. This is quite an amazing spot out here in the middle of the desert plains; it has to be one of the most strikingly unusual and distinctively beautiful small parks in the Desert Southwest.

▲ New Mexico 34

ROCK HOUND
State Park

Location: Southwest New Mexico southeast of Deming.

Access: From Interstate 10 Exit 82 at midtown Deming, travel south for 5.4 miles on New Mexico State Highway 11 to milepost 30 +.1; turn east onto a paved, local (unsigned) road and proceed east for 6 miles; turn north (left) into the park, then 0.1 mile farther to the camp/picnic area. (Signs in Deming route visitors through the east end of town then on a back road to the park, but the access is longer, less direct and more confusing.)

Day Use Facilities: Medium-sized camp/picnic area with shared facilities, plus a small group ramada; also a medium-sized picnic area and a group ramada are in the Spring Canyon section of the park, 2 miles southeast.

Overnight Facilities: 29 camp/picnic sites, all with electrical hookups, in 1 large loop; sites are very spacious, with minimal separation; parking pads are gravel, very long pull-throughs; most pads will probably require some additional leveling; tent-pitching is possible, but space is limited and sloped; sites have small ramadas (sun shelters); barbecue grills; b-y-o firewood; water at several faucets; restrooms with showers; holding tank disposal station; gravel driveway; adequate+ services are available in Deming.

Activities & Attractions: Rockhounding (up to 15 pounds per person, but you may need to be an expert or be lucky to uncover a real 'find'); foot trails; playground.

Natural Features: Located on a westward-facing hillside near the northern end of the Little Florida Mountains; the park is landscaped with small cactus and other low-level desert plants, plus lots and lots of rocks (of course); starkly barren mountains and desert plains are visible in all directions from this lofty location; typically breezy; park area is 250 acres; elevation 4500´.

Season & Fees: Open all year; please see Appendix for standard New Mexico state park entry and campground fees.

Mail & Phone: Rock Hound State Park, P.O. Box 1064, Deming, NM 88030; ☎ (505) 546-6182.

Park Notes: This is thirsty country around here. There's not enough natural shade to cast a shadow on a skink. From October to April, though, the park reportedly hosts a capacity crowd nearly every night. (Average daytime temps in the summer are consistently in the low 100's, but during the winter months they're about 30 degrees milder; it gets cool to frigid every night, year 'round.) Rock Hound achieved a reputation for being the first public park in the country to suspend the "take only pictures, leave only footprints" directive found elsewhere. (But rocks and minerals are the *only* items you can pack off from here.) Not many visitors spend a lot of time poking around the hillsides—most of them are just respectable loafers. The desert panoramas are incredibly vast.

▲ New Mexico 35 ♿

PANCHO VILLA
State Park

Location: Southwest corner of New Mexico south of Deming.

Access: From New Mexico State Highway 9 at milepost 87 +.95 (0.1 mile west of the junction of Highway 9 & State Highway 11 in the village of Columbus), turn south/southeast into the park entrance; proceed easterly for 0.1 mile, then turn south (right) for 0.2 mile to the picnic/camping area.

Day Use Facilities: Large picnic/camp area; 2 large group ramadas; drinking water; restrooms; parking at sites and in several additional small areas.

Overnight Facilities: 61 camp/picnic sites, most with partial hookups; sites are medium to very large, level, with nominal to fair separation; parking pads are gravel, mostly super long pull-throughs; adequate space for medium to large tents; ramadas (sun shelters) for all sites; fire rings; b-y-o firewood; water at sites; restrooms with solar showers; holding tank disposal station; paved perimeter driveway, gravel sub-drives within the camp area; gas and groceries+ are available in Columbus.

Activities & Attractions: Small visitor center/museum with cavalry memorabilia, photographs, and a historical film about the infamous Columbus Raid of Mexican guerrilla General Francisco "Pancho" Villa, and the U.S. retaliatory expedition led by General John J. Pershing; also, several exterior displays, informational placards, and remnants related to the Columbus Raid and subsequent U.S. operations, including the first grease rack used to lube the Army's mechanized equipment; (Check the oil too, Mack?); also, the site of the first operational military airbase (just opposite the main park on the east side of Highway 11); playground.

Natural Features: Located in a desert garden on an immense desert plain; park landscaping consists mostly of hundreds of humongous prickly pear cacti, plus medium to large hardwoods, mesquite, ocotillo, yucca, and a few evergreens, all of which provide light to light-medium shade/shelter for the sites; surrounded by near and distant mountains, including a distinctive trio of symmetrical peaks a few miles north of the park called the *Tres Hermanas* ('Three Sisters'); park area is 63 acres; elevation 4100´.

Season & Fees: Open all year; please see Appendix for standard New Mexico state park entry and campground fees.

Mail & Phone: Pancho Villa State Park, P.O. Box 224, Columbus, NM 88029; ☎ (505) 531-2711.

Park Notes: In the pre-dawn hours of March 9, 1916, some 1000 Mexican outlaws, led by self-proclaimed General of the Revolution Pancho Villa, attacked Camp Furlong, a U.S. Army post which formerly stood on the site of the present state park. After being repelled from the cavalry camp by U.S. troops' machine gun fire, the *banditos* ransacked and burned downtown Columbus. Under heavy fire and pursued by the cavalry, Villa's villains vamoosed across the international border. (Hey, this isn't Hollywood—this is twentieth century history!) Villa's brazen attack turned out to be his undoing, though. More than a third of his band of brigands were killed or wounded as a result of the ill-conceived assault.

The following day, President Woodrow Wilson sent a "Punitive Expedition" of 10,000 troops headed by General John "Black Jack" Pershing to break up Villa's forces by whatever means necessary. "Whatever means" included a fleet of trucks and cars, plus eight, old biplanes—the first time in American military history that motorized land vehicles and airplanes were used in combat. Pershing's troops—both horse-mounted and mechanized—joined in hot pursuit of the bad guys for the next 11 months and achieved limited success in dispersing Villa's forces.

In February 1917, as storm clouds were building in Europe, President Wilson recalled Pershing and his army back from Mexico to Columbus: they were needed on a new and far more strategic front. Pershing went on to command U.S. Forces in Europe during World War I; Villa eventually was persuaded (read: paid-off) by the Mexican president to 'retire', and later was assasinated. The Expedition had not only glimpsed the dawn of a new era in military operations, but it also saw the end of an age: the last use of traditional mounted cavalry in action. To some visitors, it seems odd, perhaps even a little ironic, that the park should be named after the foreign villain of the Columbus episode rather than for the American veterans who fought here. What do you think?

 New Mexico ▲

Southeast Desert & Lllano Estacado

▲ **New Mexico 36** &

OLIVER LEE MEMORIAL
State Park

Location: South-central New Mexico south of Alamogordo.

Access: From U.S. Highway 54 at milepost 55 +.8 (9 miles south of Alamogordo, 56 miles north of the New Mexico-Texas border north of El Paso), turn east onto Otero County Road A16 (Dog Canyon Road, paved); proceed 4 miles to the park entrance; turn south (right) and continue for 0.2 mile to the campground.

Day Use Facilities: Picnic tables; drinking water and restrooms in the visitor center; medium-sized parking lot.

Overnight Facilities: 43 campsites in 2 loops; sites are small, with minimal separation; parking pads are gravel, tolerably level, medium-sized, rectangular straight-ins/pull-offs; adequate space for a small to medium-sized tent in most units; ramadas (sun/wind shelters) for several sites; barbecue grills; b-y-o firewood; water at several faucets; restrooms with showers; holding tank disposal station; paved driveways; complete supplies and services are available in Alamogordo.

Activities & Attractions: Visitor center with interpretive exhibits covering the natural and cultural histories of the area; nature trails; remains of pioneer dwellings and agricultural work near the main park

area; restored Oliver Lee ranch house, 1 mile south.

Natural Features: Located on an open, westward-facing slope at the mouth of Dog Canyon (campground and visitor center) and within the canyon (historical and natural areas); park vegetation consists of an exemplary assortment of high desert plants, brush and cactus on the open slopes, and lush greenery in the canyon; the steep, barren Sacramento Mountain Escarpment looms above the park to the east; the desert lands of the vast Tularosa Valley, including White Sands, lie in full view to the west; breezy; park area is 180 acres; elevation 4500´.

Season & Fees: Open all year; $3.00 for disposal station use; please see Appendix for standard New Mexico state park entry and campground fees.

Mail & Phone: Oliver Lee Memorial State Park, 409 Dog Canyon Road, Alamogordo, NM 88310; ☎(505) 437-8284.

Park Notes: Approaching the park from the main highway, you'd never know that the dry, rugged mountains towering over the desert plain hold a hallway filled with cottonwoods, flowering plants and, would you believe, maidenhair ferns. Springs and seeps in the canyon walls and a small, all-season stream support the lush level of local vegetation, even though the region's average rain and snow fall is less than ten inches a year. For this and other practical reasons (like personal security), Dog Canyon has been inhabited for about the last 6000 years, give or take a century or two. Over 170,000 Indian artifacts—things like pieces of pottery, grinding rocks, stone knives, and the missiles of an aboriginal spear-chucking weapon called an *atlatl*—have been found within its walls.

More recent history involves the park's namesake, a native Texan who built a cattle empire in the Tularosa Valley and later went into New Mexico politics. But the park isn't entirely oriented toward history. The scenic and recreational opportunities are very good. From the campground there are some terrific views in just about any direction you care to gaze. It's usually hot during the day in summer, but generally cools down considerably after sundown. Likewise, this seems like it would make a good spot for winter sun lovers, since the unobstructed afternoon and evening rays would be felt in all campsites on the virtually treeless slope. Nonetheless, you'll still need plenty of insulation and extra warmth of one type or another—it can get doggone cold during the long winter night at the canyon of the canine.

▲ New Mexico 37

SMOKEY BEAR
Historical State Park

Location: Southeast New Mexico west of Roswell.

Access: From U.S. Highway 380 (Main Street) in midtown Capitan (1 block west of the Capitan City Hall), turn north onto Nogal Street; the visitor center and a small parking area are at the corner of Main & Nogal.

Day Use Facilities: Small picnic area; group ramada; small parking lots on the west, east and northeast sides of the park; additional, streetside parking is available.

Overnight Facilities: None; nearest public campgrounds are South Fork (Lincoln National Forest) and several City of Alamogordo camps, all near Bonito Lake, 19 miles south and west of Capitan.

Activities & Attractions: Grave of the original Smokey the Bear; interpretive trail through a botanical garden; visitor center with pertinent displays and audio-visual programs; playground; tennis court; annual Fourth of July Smokey Bear Stampede (a local event which includes a rodeo, personal appearances by Smokey, etc.); Arbor Day, tree-planting and fire prevention programs.

Natural Features: Located along the bank of Rio Salado in the Capitan Mountains; the park is landscaped with aspen, blue spruce, pinon pine and other forms of mountain vegetation; park area is 3 acres; elevation 6500´.

Season & Fees: Open all year, except for a few major holidays (daytime hours); park entry fee $0.50 per person.

Mail & Phone: Smokey Bear Historical State Park, P.O. Box 591, Capitan, NM 88316; ☎ (505) 354-2748.

Park Notes: Time: May 1950. It was a hot and dry day when someone traveling along Capitan Gap Road in Lincoln National Forest flipped a lighted cigarette or a burning match into the trees. Fanned by strong winds, the fire roared out of control and it took hundreds of fire fighters several days to overcome the blaze that blackened 17,000 acres of prime timberland. Another victim of the fire was a badly burned black bear cub found clinging to a charred tree. After receiving first aid, the cub was flown to Santa Fe for treatment by a veterinarian. His story was reported across the country and he was named "Smokey" after the famous forest fire prevention poster bear. Smokey recovered from his burns and was given another airplane ticket—this one to the National Zoo in Washington, D.C., where he spent many years as the living symbol of forest and grassland fire prevention. Although the original Smokey died some years ago and lies buried here in a boulder-marked grave on the northwest corner of the park, his successor carries on the fire-prevention message.

▲ New Mexico 38

SUMNER LAKE
State Park

Location: Eastern New Mexico south of Santa Rosa.

Access: From U.S. Highway 84 at milepost 80 +.5 (32 miles southeast of Interstate 40 Exit 277 at Santa Rosa, 11 miles north of Fort Sumner), turn west onto New Mexico State Highway 203 and proceed 5.5 miles to a point just inside the park boundary; turn north (right) onto a gravel access road to the Eastside primitive area; or continue west for another 0.5 mile to the West River and East River picnic/camp areas; or continue northerly for an additional 1.5 miles, then turn east onto a paved park access road and continue for 0.3 mile to the main park area. (Main park area is thus 7.5 miles from U.S. 84.)

Day Use Facilities: Small picnic/camp areas with vault facilities in the Eastside and River areas; medium-large picnic/camp area with shared facilities in the main area; group ramada.

Overnight Facilities: 35+ camp/picnic sites, including several with electrical hookups, in the main park area; (primitive camp/picnic sites in the Eastside area, and East and West River area are also available); sites are generally good-sized, with fair separation; parking pads are gravel, medium to long, straight-ins or pull-throughs; most pads probably will require additional leveling; large, slightly sloped and rocky, tent areas; several sites have ramadas (sun or sun/wind shelters); barbecue grills; b-y-o firewood; water at central faucets; restrooms; holding tank disposal station; paved/gravel driveways; camper supplies at a small local store; limited+ supplies and services are available in Fort Sumner.

Activities & Attractions: Fishing for stocked bass, crappie, walleye and channel catfish; boating; boat launch; playground.

Natural Features: Located on a grassy slope above the southwest shore (main area) of Sumner Lake, a 4500-acre impoundment on the Pecos River; Eastside area is on the southeast shore, River areas are along the river below the dam; some camp/picnic sites are very lightly sheltered/shaded by hardwoods and junipers; the lake is in a basin ringed by juniper-dotted, grassy slopes, surrounded by vast plains; typically breezy; elevation 4300´.

Season & Fees: Open all year, with limited facilities in winter; please see Appendix for standard New Mexico state park entry and campground fees.

Mail & Phone: Sumner Lake State Park, HC 64 Box 125, Fort Sumner, NM 88119; ☎ (505) 355-2541.

Park Notes: Colorful sunsets are almost commonplace at this park on the high plains. Remoteness and simplicity are the key words here. The nearby village of Fort Sumner is mostly famous for being the place where Sheriff Pat Garrett gunned down New York-born outlaw William H. Bonney, a.k.a. Billy the Kid.

▲ **New Mexico 39** ♿

OASIS
State Park

Location: Eastern New Mexico southwest of Clovis.

Access: From U.S. Highways 60 & 84 at milepost 384 +.6 (3 miles west of Clovis, 56 miles east of Fort Sumner), turn south onto New Mexico State Highway 467 and proceed 13 miles to milepost 3 +.9; turn west (right) onto a park access road and proceed 1.7 miles to the park entrance and the day use area, or 0.2 mile farther to the camping areas. **Alternate Access:** From U.S. Highway 70 at a point 2 miles northeast of Portales, 17 miles southwest of Clovis, turn north onto State Highway 467, proceed 4 miles to milepost 3 +.9, and continue as above.

Day Use Facilities: Small picnic area with ramadas, plus a few primitive/basic picnic/camp sites; group ramada (available to groups by reservation); drinking water; restrooms nearby; vault facilities; medium-sized parking lot.

Overnight Facilities: 11 campsites, most with electrical hookups; (a primitive camp/picnic area is also available); sites are medium to large, with fair to good separation; parking pads are gravel, medium to long pull-throughs which may require a touch of additional leveling; large areas for tents in most sites; small ramadas (sun shelters) over some table areas; barbecue grills; b-y-o firewood; water at several faucets; restrooms with showers; holding tank disposal station; gravel driveways; adequate+ supplies and services are available in Clovis or Portales.

Activities & Attractions: Fishing for stocked rainbow trout; short nature trail; ball field; playground.

Natural Features: Located around and near the shore of Oasis Lake, a 3-acre pond surrounded by plains and agricultural land; large cottonwoods provide shade/shelter for most sites; total park area is 197 acres; elevation 4200´.

Season & Fees: Open all year (principal season is April to November), with limited facilities in winter; please see Appendix for standard New Mexico state park entry and campground fees.

Mail & Phone: Oasis State Park, Route 2 Box 144, Portales, NM 88130; ☎(505) 356-5331.

Park Notes: Although we usually relate an oasis to the desert, this one is really on the high plains (which, to many travelers, are only a short step up.) The 'desert' aspect of the park is exhibited principally by its small sand dunes. There is a substantial amount of agricultural activity in the region and two good-sized towns are nearby, so this high, dry, level country appears to be quite productive. (An Air Force base and a state university help out, too.) Undoubtedly, the park's tall cottonwoods have provided shelter for many prairie-weary travelers since the original ones were planted at the turn of the century. Whoever first spoke the word "plains" probably uttered that immortal syllable somewhere along the New Mexico-Texas border.

🌲 **New Mexico 40** ♿

BOTTOMLESS LAKES
State Park

Location: Southeast New Mexico east of Roswell.

Access: From U.S. Highway 380 at milepost 165 +.7 (10 miles east of Roswell, 62 miles west of Tatum), turn south onto New Mexico State Highway 409; proceed 3.1 miles to a 3-way intersection; turn southwest (right) and continue for another 2.2 miles to the visitor center; turn east (left) onto a secondary park road and proceed east then south to viewpoints, picnic and camp areas on Cottonwood, Mirror, Devils Inkwell, Figure-8, and Pasture Lakes, and the trail to Lost Lake; or continue past the visitor center turnoff for another 1.8 miles, then turn east (left) to the main campground at Lea Lake.

Day Use Facilities: Small picnic/camp areas with shared facilities along the east side of the park road; small day use area at Lea Lake.

Overnight Facilities: *Lea Lake Campground*: 10 campsites with partial hookups; (a reservable group area is also available); sites vary from small to very large, with minimal separation; parking pads are level, gravel, short straight-ins or very long pull-throughs; enough room for small to medium-sized tents; sites have ramadas (sun shelters) over table areas; barbecue grills; b-y-o firewood; water at faucets throughout; restrooms; showers; holding tank disposal station; gravel/dirt driveways; *additional camp/picnic areas*: semi-primitive campsites are available at Mirror, Figure-8 and Pasture Lakes; sites have gravel pads, room for small tents, some sites have ramadas; water at central faucets; vault facilities; complete supplies and services are available in Roswell.

Activities & Attractions: Network of nature trails and hiking trails to several of the lakes, plus rim trails which lead to several viewpoints above the lakes; swimming permitted at Lea Lake; scuba diving permitted (check-in with the park ranger first); playground; fishing for stocked trout; limited boating/canoeing; visitor center with interpretive displays.

Natural Features: Located on the shores of 7 small "bottomless" lakes, plus "Lazy Lagoon"; reddish bluffs border the lakes on the east; small, branchy hardwoods and low-level brush provide some vegetational interest; the Pecos River flows nearby, just west of the park; surrounded by rolling plains, with mountains visible in the distant west; total park area is 1670 acres, including 60 acres of water; elevation 3500´.

Season & Fees: Open all year; please see Appendix for reservation information, standard park entry and campground fees; special day use fee for Lea Lake is $5.00 per vehicle up to 7 persons, $0.50 per person thereafter (subject to change).

Mail & Phone: Bottomless Lakes State Park, Auto Route E, Box 120, Roswell, NM 88201; ☎(505) 624-6058.

Park Notes: The Bottomless Lakes were formed when circulating water dissolved underground deposits of gypsum and salt and created a natural system of subway tunnels and mine shafts. The roofs of some of these passages collapsed and in the aftermath the 'sinkholes' filled with water. (At the risk of spoiling the 'surprise', it might be mentioned that the name "Bottomless" was coined many years ago by cowpokes who couldn't reach the bottoms of these unusually hued lakes with their longest lariats. The maximum depth of the lakes is actually about 90 feet.)

▲ New Mexico 41

HARRY McADAMS
State Park

Location: Southeast corner of New Mexico northwest of Hobbs.

Access: From New Mexico State Highway 18 at milepost 57 +.5 (6 miles northwest of Hobbs, 13 miles southeast of Lovington), turn southwest onto Jack Gomez Boulevard; proceed 0.3 mile to the state park entrance; continue for 0.3 mile around to the south end of the park to the day use area, and the campground just beyond.

Day Use Facilities: Medium-large picnic area; several ramadas (sun/wind shelters); drinking water; restrooms.

Overnight Facilities: 15 campsites with electrical hookups; sites are medium-sized, level, with minimal to nominal separation; parking pads are paved, medium to long straight-ins; spacious tent areas; half of the sites have large, adobe ramadas (sun/wind shelters); barbecue grills; b-y-o firewood; water at central faucets; restrooms with showers; holding tank disposal station; paved driveway; complete supplies and services are available in Hobbs.

Activities & Attractions: Historical exhibits relating the history and geography of the Llano Estacado in the park office; large playground.

Natural Features: Located on the high plains of the oil-rich Permian Basin; the day use area is on an expansive hardwood-and-evergreen-dotted lawn around a pair of small ponds spanned by a footbridge across a 'narrows' between them; the campground

is similarly landscaped; surrounding countryside is as flat as a billiard table (although not nearly as green); hot summers, mild winters; typically breezy; park area is 38 acres; elevation 3700´.

Season & Fees: Open all year; park entry fee $3.00 per vehicle; please see Appendix for standard New Mexico state park campground fees.

Mail & Phone: Harry McAdams State Park, 5000 State Park Road, Hobbs, NM 88240; ☎(505) 392-5845.

Park Notes: Ever since the Spanish explorers first trekked across these plains in the mid-1500's, this vast region which flanks the Eastern New Mexico-West Texas border has been known as the *Llano Estacado*. The phrase can be translated as 'Stockaded Plain' or 'Staked Plain'. The name refers to the *Llano's* great, isolated escarpments which, when viewed from a distance, resemble fortresses or stockades with outer walls made of tall pickets or stakes sunk into the earth. However, a high school history text of recent vintage, which was sold to schools around the nation by a large publishing company in the East, has its own version of the origin of the name: The book claims that "Staked Plain" was derived from a practice of the early Plains Indians of pounding stakes into the ground as they traveled in order to find their way back home. (Sure. And they carried the wood in the back of their Chevy pickups.) The park looks more like a golf course than the neighboring golf course. Very nice. This is a good, four-season recreation area. Although it occasionally does get a little chilly around here in winter, the overall climate is conducive to a fairly pleasant wintertime stop or stay.

▲ New Mexico 42 ♿

BRANTLEY LAKE
State Park

Location: Southeast corner of New Mexico north of Carlsbad.

Access: From U.S. Highway 285 at milepost 45 +.6 (at the junction of U.S. 285 & New Mexico State Highway 137, 12

miles north of Carlsbad, 24 miles south of Artesia), turn east onto Capitan Reef Road (paved for the first mile, then gravel) and travel east and north for 4.4 miles; turn west (left) onto East Brantley Lake Road (paved) and proceed 0.35 mile to the park entrance station/visitor center; continue westerly for 1.4 mile, then swing south (left) for another 0.5 mile; turn northwest (right) into the Limestone camp/picnic area.
Additional Access: From U.S. Highway 285 at milepost 48 +.6 (15 miles north of Carlsbad) turn east onto West Brantley Lake Road (paved) and proceed 1 mile to a secondary day use area.

Day Use Facilities: Medium-sized camp and picnic area with shared facilities at Limestone; undeveloped secondary day use area on the west side of the lake.

Overnight Facilities: *Limestone Campground*: 51 camp/picnic sites with partial hookups; sites are small+ to medium-sized, with nominal to fair separation; parking pads are paved, medium to medium+ straight-ins; many pads will require a little additional leveling; adequate space for medium to large tents on a gravel surface; ramadas (sun shelters) for most sites; barbecue grills; b-y-o firewood; water at sites; restrooms with showers; holding tank disposal station; paved driveways; complete supplies and services are available in Carlsbad.

Activities & Attractions: Boating; boat launch; fishing for standard warm-water species; small visitor center.

Natural Features: Located on a small ridge/knoll on a stark, high desert plain above Brantley Lake, an impoundment on the Pecos River; camp/picnic sites receive minimal to light shade from medium-sized hardwoods; natural vegetation throughout the park consists of clump grass and small brush; small hills lie nearby, the Guadalupe Mountains rise in the distant southwest; total park land area is 2,000 acres (although only a small portion will be developed; total water area (if/when the reservoir is filled to capacity) is 12,000 acres; elevation 3300´.

Season & Fees: Open all year; please see Appendix for standard New Mexico state park entry and campground fees.

Mail & Phone: Brantley Lake State Park, P.O. Box 2288, Carlsbad, NM 88221; ☎(505) 457-2384.

Park Notes: Considering the local natural environment, the park landscaping's simple improvements on nature are probably quite welcome to most visitors. Limestone is the only public campground around here which conveniently serves visitors to nearby Carlsbad Caverns. (Carlsbad Caverns doesn't have a campground; the only other public camp for many miles is Dog Canyon, a comparatively primitive spot in Guadalupe Mountains National Park, at the south end of New Mexico State Highway 137, just south of the New Mexico-Texas border.) Most of the facilities at Brantley's Limestone unit have been constructed fairly recently.

🌲 **New Mexico 43** ♿

LIVING DESERT
Zoological & Botanical State Park

Location: Southeast corner of New Mexico on the northwest edge of Carlsbad.

Access: From U.S. Highway 285 in the northwest corner of Carlsbad (near the Guadalupe Medical Center), turn west onto Mills Drive and proceed west and south for 0.7 mile; a few yards after the road curves south, turn east (left) into the park.

Day Use Facilities: None; nearest picnic area is in a large Carlsbad city park on the east side of the main highway a mile southeast of the state park turnoff; drinking water, restrooms and large parking lot in the state park.

Overnight Facilities: None; nearest public campground is in Brantley Dam State Park.

Activities & Attractions: Trails past living exhibits of desert fauna and flora in a natural setting including large mammals, a prairie dog town, birds of prey, an aviary and a duck pond; greenhouse with succulent plants from around the world; visitor center with interpretive displays related to Chihuahuan desert geology, archaeology, history, animals, and use and conservation of natural resources; special events such as the annual Mescal Roast (see Park Notes), gem and mineral shows, Indian and Southwest art shows.

Natural Features: Located in the Ocotillo Hills; park vegetation/landscaping consists of a tremendous variety of Chihuahuan Desert plants, brush, cactus and other succulents; bordered by vast plains to the north, east and south; the Sacramento Mountains and the Guadalupe Mountains rise to the west and southwest; park area is 1120 acres; elevation 3200´.

Season & Fees: Open all year, except for a few major holidays (hours vary seasonally); please see Appendix for standard New Mexico state park entry fees (group tour rates are also available).

Mail & Phone: Living Desert State Park, P.O. Box 100, Carlsbad, NM 88220; ☎(505) 887-5516.

Park Notes: Living Desert is on the New Mexico "Don't Miss It" list. Sure, almost everybody who visits this region takes the underground tour in Carlsbad Caverns NP; after a few hours spent chasing stalactites and stalagmites and dodging bats in the caverns' clammy coolness, many travelers move on down the highway. Those who bypass Living Desert don't know what they're missing. This park has what might be the most comprehensive collection of desert plants and animals in the Southwest. (Boyce Thompson Southwest Arboretum in the Arizona state park system has a super assortment of desert plants, but its animal population consists of whatever happens to be in the neighborhood.) Plan on an absolute minimum of one hour to walk through the park. Every year in May, Living Desert hosts a 'Mescal Roast' which is reported to have grown tremendously in popularity in recent years. The weekend fest includes Indian 'Spirit Dances' and other Southwest-style activities. Mescal, the heart of the *agave* or 'century plant', is a traditional food of the Mescalero Apaches. The mescal is toasted to perfection in roasting pits for four days before it's ready to be sampled. Is it a savory snack? Let's just say that a fondness for mescal is an "acquired taste".

* * * * *

Several former state parks are still listed in quite a few pieces of travel and promotional literature, although they no longer are officially part of the New Mexico state park system. The onetime state parks and their new caretakers are:

Indian Petroglyphs (Albuquerque): Has become part of Petroglyphs National Monument

Kit Carson Memorial (Taos): City of Taos

Red Rock (east of Gallup): City of Gallup

Rio Bravo (Albuquerque): City of Albuquerque

Rio Grand Gorge (southwest of Taos): Bureau of Land Management, U.S. Department of the Interior

San Gabriel (Albuquerque): City of Albuquerque

Shooting Range (west of Albuquerque): City of Albuquerque

Valley of Fires (west of Carrizozo): Bureau of Land Management, U.S. Department of the Interior

According to New Mexico governmental sources, the transfer of the former state parks to other entities was the result of the policy of a prior administration. A previous New Mexico governor is reported to have been a strong advocate of the shift of responsibility for parks and recreation away from the state level and toward local and national government and private enterprise. It is said that recent administrations administrations have been more moderate in this matter.

Utah State Parks

Dead Horse Point State Park

 Utah 🏕

Greater Salt Lake Valley

🌲 **Utah 1** ♿

BEAR LAKE:
MARINA
State Park

Location: North-central corner of Utah northeast of Logan.

Access: From U.S. Highway 89 at milepost 413 (1 mile north of Garden City, 2.5 miles south of the Utah-Idaho border near Fishaven, Idaho), turn east into the park.

Day Use Facilities: Medium-sized picnic area; group pavilion; drinking water and restrooms in the visitor center; medium-sized parking lot.

Overnight Facilities: 15 campsites in a paved parking lot arrangement; sites are very small, essentially level, with fender to fender parking slots; adequate space for a small tent in most sites; fire rings; b-y-o firewood; water at central faucets; restrooms with showers at the visitor center; holding tank disposal station; gas and groceries are available in Garden City and Fishaven.

Activities & Attractions: Boating; sailing; boat launch; marina; rock jetties form a small artificial harbor; fishing for cutthroat and mackinaw trout; dip-netting for the smelt-like Cisco during its January run; watching for the legendary Bear Lake Monster, a serpentine creature said by Indians and early settlers (and knowledgeable contemporary locals) to inhabit the depths of the lake; swimming.

Natural Features: Located on a small bay on the west shore of Bear Lake; park vegetation consists of a strip of watered grass between the camping lot and the rocky beach, and hardwoods which provide mostly early morning shade; high, partially forested, dryish mountains parallel the east shore of the lake, more-forested mountains rise to the west; Bear Lake covers 71,000 acres; elevation 5900´.

Season & Fees: Open all year, with limited services November to May; please see Appendix for reservation information and standard Utah state park entry and campground fees.

Mail & Phone: Bear Lake State Park, P.O. Box 184, Garden City, UT 84028-0184; ☎ (435) 946-3343.

Park Notes: This section of Bear Lake State Park seems to be used principally by boaters and transient rv campers. (Although the individual campsites are very small, a large tent could be pitched with the cooperation of neighboring campers if they didn't mind some encroachment on their own slice of rented turf.) The camping area is right along the main access driveway to the harbor facilities, so local traffic may pass within a few inches of your hood ornament. Really nice lake views from here, though. The little harbor seems to be a favorite of sailboaters. Winterwise, there are a few things to do around here, even though the lake is frozen-over. The most popular pastime is dip-netting through the ice for the Bonneville Cisco, a unique species of whitefish found in Bear Lake.

▲ Utah 2 &

BEAR LAKE:
RENDEZVOUS BEACH
State Park

Location: North-central corner of Utah northeast of Logan.

Access: From Utah State Highway 30 at milepost 124 +.5 (2 miles northwest of Laketown, 8 miles south of the junction of Highway 30 and U.S. Highway 89 at Garden City), turn north to the park entrance; turn east onto the main park road and proceed 0.5 mile to an intersection; go north (left) on the beach road for 0.2 mile to Willow; or turn north/east directly into the Cottonwood area; or continue east for another 0.2 mile past Cottonwood to the Big Creek area.

Day Use Facilities: Medium-sized picnic area; restrooms; large parking area.

Overnight Facilities: *Cottonwood Campground*: 60 campsites; sites are in a paved, parking lot arrangement, very small, level, with nil separation; parking spaces are short straight-ins; room for tents around the perimeter of the camping lot; fire rings; water at central faucets; restrooms with showers; paved driveway; *Willow Campground*: 32 campsites; sites are in a paved parking lot arrangement, very small, level, with nil separation; parking spaces are short, wide straight-ins; fire rings; restrooms; paved driveway; *Big Creek Campground*: 45 campsites, including some with full hookups; sites are small to medium-sized, generally level, with minimal to fairly good separation; parking pads are paved, mostly medium-length straight-ins; adequate space for medium to large tents in most units; fire rings or barbecue grills; water at faucets throughout; restrooms; paved driveways; b-y-o firewood is recommended for all three campgrounds; holding tank disposal station in the Cottonwood section; gas and groceries are available in Laketown and Garden City.

Activities & Attractions: Long, sandy beach; swimming permitted; boating; boat launch.

Natural Features: Located on the south shore of Bear Lake; in the Cottonwood area a line of large cottonwoods between the sites and the water's edge provides shade/shelter for some tent areas, although most parking slots are on the sunny side; expansive, grassy sections border the Cottonwood area; Willow area campsites are somewhat wind-sheltered by small trees and large bushes, but have minimal shade; in the Big Creek area about half of the sites are along or near the beach, and are sheltered/shaded by large hardwoods; remainder of the sites are behind the beach on an open flat; Big Creek flows past the west end of the campground; high mountains, mostly covered by sage and crunchgrass but with some timber at the higher elevations, border the lake east and west; elevation 5900´.

Season & Fees: May to November; please see Appendix for reservation information and standard Utah state park entry and campground fees.

Mail & Phone: Bear Lake State Park, P.O. Box 184, Garden City, UT 84028-0184; ☎ (435) 946-3343.

Park Notes: Most picnic spots and camp areas may not be much, but you came here to enjoy the lake and the beach, and not to sit at a table or around the fire, right? Although the sites themselves may not be exceptional, the surroundings are really quite nice. Of the several camping areas on Bear Lake, Big Creek is, with little doubt, the nicest. About half of the campsites are shoreside or very close to the lake shore, and have terrific views of the long, narrow valley in which the lake is located. (During the summer, it might be worth considering getting a campsite reservation for a weekend spot at Big Creek—and maybe even for a weekday if you won't be arriving until late in the day—then hope you'll be assigned to a good site.)

In addition to the developed campgrounds at Bear Lake Marina and Rendezvous Beach, there is also a primitive camp area and boat ramp in the park's Eastside section, on the

East Lake Road, 10 miles north of Lakeside. It's in the vicinity of the deepest part of the lake—a hole that's 208 feet deep. (Maybe that's where the Bear Lake Monster hides out.)

▲ Utah 3 ♿

HYRUM
State Park

Location: North-central Utah south of Logan.

Access: From the junction of U.S. Highways 89/91 and Utah State Highway 101 just east of Wellsville, turn east onto Highway 101; proceed east for 2.4 miles to milepost 3 +.7 on the west edge of the community of Hyrum; turn south (right) onto 4th Street West and continue for 0.9 mile (you'll pass the South Cache Middle School on the right) to the main park entrance; proceed through the parking lot, then turn west (right) into the west (main) camping area, or east toward the east camping section; or from just outside the park entrance, turn east (left) and follow the signed route to the beach area. (Note: this is the access that most likely would be used by most travelers; access is also possible by taking Main Street in Hyrum west to 4th Street West, and then turning south for 0.4 mile to the park.)

Day Use Facilities: Small picnic area; drinking water; restrooms; medium-sized parking lot for picnic area, medium-sized parking lot for beach area.

Overnight Facilities: 39 campsites in 2 main sections; (a large group camp area is also available); 24 sites in the west section are small, level, with minimal separation; parking areas are small, gravel, straight-ins/pull-offs; large, grassy tent areas; 15 sites in the east section are in a paved parking lot arrangement, with a few adjacent tables; barbecue grills; b-y-o firewood; water at several faucets; restrooms with showers, plus auxiliary vault facilities; gravel/paved driveways; limited supplies and services are available in Hyrum, 1 mile east.

Activities & Attractions: Swimming beach; fishing; boating; boat launch and docks; volleyball courts.

Natural Features: Located on the north shore of Hyrum Lake, a 450-acre reservoir near the foothills of the Wasatch Range; picnic and camp areas are on a bluff above the lake shore; picnic area and west camping area have watered and mown lawns, and hardwoods which provide some shelter/shade in most sites; east camping section has hardwoods along the perimeter which provide a small amount of shelter for most parking spaces; elevation 4800´.

Season & Fees: April to November; please see Appendix for reservation information and standard Utah state park entry and campground fees.

Mail & Phone: Hyrum State Park, 405 West 300 South, Hyrum, UT 84319; ☎ (435) 245-6866.

Park Notes: Most of the picnic and camp sites have terrific mountain and lake views because of their elevated, open location. Much of the mountain country around this man-made lake can be seen from this spot. The local geography must have looked quite a bit different back in 1825 when Jim Bridger, Jedediah Smith, William Sublette and other historic notables cached 75 bales of beaver pelts near the site of the present-day park. Back then the furs had a street value of about $150,000 when they were finally marketed in St. Louis.

▲ Utah 4

WILLARD BAY:
NORTH
State Park

Location: North-central Utah north of Ogden.

Access: From Interstate 15 Exit 360 for Willard (6 miles south of Brigham City, 14 miles north of Ogden), proceed to the west side of the freeway, then south on the park access road for 0.1 mile to the park entrance station; the campground is to the west (right), just beyond the entrance; the day use area is 0.7 mile south of the entrance station.

Day Use Facilities: Medium-sized picnic area; several small and medium-sized ramadas (sun shelters); drinking water; restrooms/bathhouse with showers; large parking lot; concession stand.

Overnight Facilities: 61 campsites; (a group use area with large shelter is also available); sites are medium-sized, level, with minimal to fair separation; most parking pads are long, paved, tandem pull-throughs (i.e., two sites share the same parking space); good-sized tent areas; barbecue grills; b-y-o firewood; water at several faucets; restrooms with showers; holding tank disposal station; paved driveways; gas and groceries in Willard, 1 mile east; adequate to complete supplies and services are available in Brigham City and Ogden.

Activities & Attractions: Swimming beach; boating; boat launch and docks; marina; fishing for walleye, crappie and channel catfish.

Natural Features: Located on the east shore of 15.5-square mile Willard Reservoir, in the Great Salt Lake Valley; picnic sites are along the lake shore and are lightly sheltered/shaded by scattered hardwoods; many campsites are in an open setting, although some are sheltered/shaded by large hardwoods and dense bushes; watered, mown grass in and around some picnic and camp sites, plus sections of mown and unmown natural grass, marsh, and stands of hardwoods in adjacent areas; dense vegetation around the campground's "Duck Pond" (marsh) and along Willow Creek, which flows past the campground; the high, rocky Wasatch Range rises sharply from the valley floor, just to the east; the desert Promontory Mountains are visible across the lake, in the distant west, on Promontory Point (Peninsula), a 30-mile-long landmass which extends southward from the north end of the Great Salt Lake; elevation 4200´.

Season & Fees: Open all year, with limited services November to April; campsite reservations accepted; please see Appendix for reservation information and standard Utah state park entry and campground fees.

Mail & Phone: Willard Bay State Park, 900 West 650 North, Box A, Willard, UT 84340; ☎ (435) 734-9494.

Park Notes: Willard Bay originally was part of the salt marsh of Great Salt Lake; but in the middle 1960's, a 14.5-mile-long, 35´-high dike was built around the lakeside perimeter of the bay by the Bureau of Reclamation. Runoff water from the Wasatch Range eventually filled the newly created impoundment, and the dike thus serves as a man-made barrier reef which separates salt water from fresh water. Water from the 9900-acre reservoir is used principally for crop irrigation. (The numerous orchards in this region make up what is locally called "Utah's Fruitway".)

▲ Utah 5 ♿

WILLARD BAY:
SOUTH
State Park

Location: North-central Utah north of Ogden.

Access: From Interstate 15 Exit 354 (8 miles north of Ogden, 12 miles south of Brigham City), go to the west side of the freeway, then turn south onto Utah State Highway 126, and parallel I-15 for 0.2 mile (to the Box Elder-Weber county line); turn west onto 4000 North Street; proceed west for 1.3 miles, then turn north (right, immediately after the railroad tracks); follow this road for 0.9 mile, then turn west (left) again and continue for 0.2 mile to the park entrance station; at a point 0.4 mile beyond the entrance station, turn south for 0.2 mile to the park (for a total of 3 miles from the Interstate).

Day Use Facilities: Good-sized camp/picnic area with shared facilities; large parking lot.

Overnight Facilities: 20 camp/picnic sites; sites are primarily park 'n walk units, with tables and fire facilities along the perimeter of a large, paved parking area; designated tent section at the west end has adequate space for several large tents on a grassy surface; entire area is level, and sites are generally well-spaced; small ramadas (sun shelters) over some table areas; fire rings;

b-y-o firewood; water at central faucets; restrooms with showers; camper supplies at the marina; complete supplies and services are available in Ogden.

Activities & Attractions: Boating; boat launch; marina; fishing.

Natural Features: Located on the edge of a level plain at the southeast corner of 9900-acre Willard Reservoir in the Great Salt Lake Valley; park vegetation consists of watered, mown lawns, and small to large hardwoods which provide some shade/shelter for many sites; a marsh area is adjacent; high, rocky peaks of the Wasatch Range are in full view to the east, desert mountains rise in the distant west; elevation 4200´.

Season & Fees: Open all year, with limited services November to April; please see Appendix for reservation information and standard Utah state park entry and campground fees.

Mail & Phone: Willard Bay State Park, 650 North 900 West Box A, Willard, UT 84340; ☎(435) 734-9494.

Park Notes: While this area hasn't quite the level of facilities of its sister section (also see info on Willard Bay North), it is also less popular, and hence a bit more likely to have a weekend picnic or camp site available for late arrivals. It is said that Willard Bay's proximity to the valley's metro areas and its commensurately high level of usage help it to be one of the relatively few state parks in Utah with fee revenues that equal its operating budget.

▲ Utah 6 ⑬

FORT BUENAVENTURA
State Park

Location: North-central Utah in Ogden.

Access: From Interstate 15 Exit 345 on the west end of Ogden, travel east on Utah State Highway 53/24th Street for 0.9 mile; turn south (right) onto A Avenue for 0.05 mile, then swing east/southeast (left) onto James Brown Drive; continue southerly (past the Miles Goodyear athletic complex) for 0.25 mile to the park entrance; proceed ahead for a final 0.2 mile to the parking lot and day use areas.

Day Use Facilities: Medium-sized picnic area; drinking water; restrooms; medium-sized parking lot.

Overnight Facilities: Group tent camping area (available by reservation only); nearest public campground available to individuals is in Willard Bay State Park.

Activities & Attractions: Replicas of the log stockade and cabin on the site of the original fort; paved trails; canoeing (canoe rentals); limited fishing.

Natural Features: Located along the banks of the Weber River in the Great Salt Lake Valley; park vegetation consists of medium to dense stands of hardwoods, brush, and sections of mown grass; a small impoundment on the river serves as a canoeing pond; the Wasatch Range, to the east, is partially visible from the park; park area is 32 acres; elevation 4500´.

Season & Fees: April to November; please see Appendix for standard Utah state park entry fee.

Mail & Phone: Fort Buenaventura State Park, 2450 A Avenue, Ogden, UT 84401; ☎(385) 621-4808.

Park Notes: Fort Buenaventura was founded by trapper Miles Goodyear in the mid-1840's, and is generally acknowledged to be the first permanent Anglo-American settlement in the Great Basin. The region originally was claimed by Spain, then independent Mexico. In the early 1840's, the Mexican government deeded the real estate between the Wasatch Range and the Great Salt Lake to mountain man Goodyear. Nowadays, the park hosts the annual Mountain Man Rendezvous, which sees participants dressed in nineteenth century clothing, toting muzzleloaders and other authentic gear, and partaking in period pastimes.

▲ Utah 7 ♿

ANTELOPE ISLAND
State Park

Location: North-central Utah southwest of Ogden.

Access: From Interstate 15 Exit 335 for Freeport Center & Syracuse, (12 miles south of Ogden, 24 miles north of Salt Lake City) head west on Utah State Highway 108 (Antelope Road) for 4 miles; continue west on Utah State Highway 127 for 2.9 miles to the east terminus of the Antelope Island Causeway; travel west on the causeway for another 7 miles to the island and the park.

Day Use Facilities: Large picnic area; shelters; group picnic areas with pavilions; drinking water; restrooms; several parking areas.

Overnight Facilities: 75 campsites; (a group camp area is also available, by reservation); sites are small+ to medium-sized, with nominal separation; parking pads are gravel, mostly medium-length straight-ins; adequate space for tents; fire rings; b-y-o firewood;water at several faucets; restrooms with showers, plus auxiliary vaults; holding tank disposal station; gravel driveways; complete supplies and services are available near the Interstate interchange.

Activities & Attractions: Swimming and wading; boating; boat launch; interpretive center; biking.

Natural Features: Located on the shore at the northeast tip of 28,000-acre Antelope Island, the largest isle in the Great Salt Lake; a spinal column of rugged, high and dry mountains covers most of the island, although the park itself is on a somewhat more-level section; vegetation consists mainly of dry range grass; elevation 4200´.

Season & Fees: Open all year,with limited services in winter; 14 day limit; please see Appendix for reservation information and standard Utah state park entry and campground fees.

Mail & Phone: Antelope Island State Park, 4528 West 1700 South, Syracuse, UT 84075; ☎(801) 773-2941 or ☎(801) 725-9263.

Park Notes: Antelope Island is the largest isle in the Great Salt Lake. During the Great Salt Lake's high-water period of the mid-1980's, the lake rose nearly a dozen feet above its usual level and its surface area swelled from 1000 square miles to 2500 square miles. Because this park is situated along a low shoreline, most of the facilities were inundated and damaged or completely wiped-out. After the floodwaters had receded, the buckled and broken, two-lane causeway to the island looked as if it had been used for armored tank maneuvers and artillery practice. Most of the park's facilities had to be rebuilt. Ditto the causeway. Meanwhile, the island's buffalo herd, an assortment of other wild critters, and the thousand or so cattle which are barged-in for winter grazing, had Antelope Island's treeless shores and slopes pretty much to themselves.

▲ Utah 8

GREAT SALT LAKE
State Park

Location: North-central Utah west of Salt Lake City.

Access: From Interstate 80 Exit 104 for Saltair Drive/Magna (16 miles west of Salt Lake City), proceed 0.15 mile to the north side of the freeway and a 'T' intersection; turn east (right) onto a gravel frontage road and proceed 1.9 miles; turn north (left) into the park.

Day Use Facilities: Several randomly placed picnic tables; drinking water; restrooms/bathhouses; very large parking lot.

Overnight Facilities: None; nearest public campground is in Utah Lake State Park.

Activities & Attractions: Beachcombing; wading/swimming; boating (marina adjacent); (reportedly, beach parties are also favorite, albeit unofficial, activities).

Natural Features: Located on a beach/flat along the south shore of the Great Salt Lake; except for a few patches of wild grass, the park is virtually devoid of vegetation; high, desert mountains are visible in several directions, as is the Wasatch Range to the east; elevation 4200´.

Season & Fees: Open all year; please see Appendix for standard Utah state park entry fee.

Mail & Phone: Great Salt Lake State Park, P.O. Box 323, Magna, UT 84044; ☎(801) 533-4080.

Park Notes: Try to imagine the worst ocean beach you've ever seen. Well, *that* one is several notches higher on the list of preferred places than *this* one. An official in another Utah park put it this way: "If the smell doesn't get to you, the brine flies probably will". The multi-smoke-stacked smelter which forms the southern backdrop for the park isn't exactly picture post card perfect either. And then there's the bizarre, flooded-out resort next door to the park: the onion-domed, Turkish Delight architecture of the doomed spa contrasts markedly with the surrounding terrain. Or does it? For the local landscape might indeed resemble the desolate coast of the Persian Gulf or along the Suez Canal.

So why would you want to make a trip to this spot, or even stop-by if you're comfortably cruising along on slate-level I-80? Well, one traveler's pit is another visitor's prize, and the experience offered here approaches a level of distinctiveness that's nearly unmatched anywhere else in the country. (The Salton Sea region of the Southern California desert is comparable— although its scale is not quite as immense and its reputation not quite as widespread.) A lot of people get a kick out of trying out the lake's waters to see just how 'unsinkable' they really are. Depending largely upon the amount of runoff water which dilutes the salt content, the lake's salinity can be anywhere from two to five times higher than that of the ocean, so a body's 'float factor' is pretty good. The annual precipitation will also determine the distance from the parking lot to the shore— the water's edge could be a few feet to several hundred yards away. Massive, mountainous, desolate-looking, and yet intriguingly handsome, Antelope Island will be plainly visible off the starboard bow

when your parked vehicle is faced 'seaward'. Now, about those brine flies.....

🔺 **Utah 9** ♿

JORDAN RIVER
State Park

Location: North-central Utah in Salt Lake City.

Access: From the junction of Interstate Highways 80 & 215 on the west side of Salt Lake City, (for areas along the *west* bank of the river): take the Redwood Road Exit (Exit 118 off I-80 or Exit 22 off I-215) to Redwood Road (Utah State Highway 68); travel north on Redwood Road for 0.6 mile to Cottonwood Park, or an additional 1.4 miles to the park office, or another 0.3 mile to the golf course, all on the east (right) side of the road.

Alternate Access: From the junction of Interstate Highways 80 & 15, (for areas along the *east* bank of the river): take the exit for 9th West (900 West) Street (Exit 120 off I-80 or Exit 311 off I-15); go south on 9th West for 0.9 mile to 8th South Park; or continue for another 1.2 miles south on 9th West, then west on 17th South (1700 South) Street for 1 block to the Jogging & Exercise Course; or from the Interstate exit go north on 9th West for 0.4 mile to North Temple, then west on North Temple for 0.3 mile to the hike/bike trailhead (near the state fair grounds).

Day Use Facilities: Picnic areas with pavilions (sun shelters), drinking water, restrooms and parking lots at: Cottonwood Park, (on North Star Drive, 1 block east of Redwood Road behind the Department of Agriculture building); 800 South Park (9th West & Genessee Avenue); and at the Jogging & Exercise Course (north off of 17th South, a block west of 9th West).

Overnight Facilities: None; nearest public campground is in East Canyon State Park; (easiest and quickest campground to reach is in Utah Lake State Park).

Activities & Attractions: (Listed north to south): ohv (off-highway vehicle) training center with classrooms, for individuals ages 8-16 (west of Redwood Road near I-215

Exit 28, call the park office for enrollment details); model airplane port with surfaced runway (a half-mile south of the ohv area); golf course (9 holes, par 3); tennis court at the golf course; wheelchair exercise course (just north of Cottonwood Park, on the east side of the river, accessible via a bridge from the main park); large playground and grassy field at Cottonwood Park; 1.5-mile paved hiking, jogging, bicycling trail along the east side of the river from North Temple to 10th North; equestrian trail along the west side of the river from North Temple to 17th North; Jogging and Exercise Course with training stations on a large, grassy field; soccer field at the J & E Course; limited boating, canoeing, floating; small boat launch/dock areas about every mile or so along the river, most of them accessible from side streets; limited fishing (mostly for stocked catfish); certain pavilions are reservable by groups.

Natural Features: Located in an 8.5 mile stretch along the banks of the Jordan River in the Great Salt Lake Valley; vegetation in developed park areas consists of watered, mown lawns and some large and small hardwoods; natural areas along the riverbank have large hardwoods, plus some brush and grass; the Jordan River rises from its headwaters in Utah Lake and lazily drifts north through the valley until it exits into the Great Salt Lake; the lofty, rugged Wasatch Range rises sharply to the east and is visible from most park areas; the ribbon of greenery along the riverbanks is also locally known as the "Jordan River Parkway"; elevation 4200´.

Season & Fees: Open all year; $5.00 for 9 holes of golf; $4.00 for the model port; please contact the park for ohv center fees; (no fees for the use of other facilities, subject to change).

Mail & Phone: Jordan River State Park, 1084 North Redwood Road, Salt Lake City, UT 84116; ☎(801) 533-4496 (office); or ☎(801) 533-4527 (golf course).

Park Notes: If you glance at your Utah highway map, you'll see a large 'H' pattern of interstate highways near midtown Salt Lake City. Interstates 15 and 215 form the north-south uprights of the 'H'; Interstate 80 connects the centers of the uprights in an east-west line. The park lies totally within the 'H', and is bisected by I-80. Thus, most of the various park sections are only a couple of minutes' drive from one of the freeways.

Another way of envisioning the layout here is to just remember that the majority of the park units are acccessible from three main city streets: Redwood Road, North Temple and 9th West. (Once you're off the freeway, the simplest way to get from the park units on the west bank to those on the east bank is to use North Temple.) In essence, this is a chain of city parks operated and funded by the state park system. But even if you're just passin' through town, you might want to swing off the Interstate and use one or more of the park units to play a round of golf or shoot some hoops or stretch your travel-cricked legs.

▲ Utah 10 ♿

THIS IS THE PLACE
State Park

Location: North-central Utah on the east edge of Salt Lake City.

Access: From the intersection of Utah State Highway 186 (Foothill Drive) and Sunnyside Avenue (in the southeast corner of Salt Lake City, 2.5 miles northwest of Interstate 80 Exit 129) proceed east on Sunnyside Avenue for 0.3 mile; turn northeast (left) onto the park access road and proceed 0.4 mile to the main park area. (Note: If you're approaching the city on I-80 from the west, or you're on I-15 northbound or southbound, the simplest way to find the park is to pick up I-80 East and head on out to Exit 129, then northwest on Utah 186 (Foothill Drive); other accesses might look good on the highway map, but you'll get the grand tour of Salt Lake City and have to thread your way through town in a half-dozen miles of stop-and-go traffic.)

Day Use Facilities: Small picnic area just above the visitor center; large (group) picnic area below the monument; drinking water; restrooms; large parking lot.

Overnight Facilities: None; nearest public campground is in East Canyon State Park.

Activities & Attractions: This is the Place Monument; visitor center with a three-walled mural depicting the 1300-mile Mormon emigration and a souvenir shop; Old Deseret, a 'living history museum', consisting of 12 renovated original buildings or authentic replicas of old structures, including Brigham Young's farmhouse, houses and cabins of several other early pioneers, a carpenter's shop and a social hall (guide pamphlet available); demonstrations of pioneer lifestyles and crafts are given by costumed personnel during the summer; sections of the Mormon Pioneer Trail, a designated National Historic Trail, which begins on the east bank of the Mississippi River in Nauvoo, Illinois and terminates in Salt Lake City (guide pamphlet/map available).

Natural Features: Located in the foothills of the Wasatch Range at the west end of Emigration Canyon above Salt Lake City; park vegetation consists of large sections of mown lawns dotted with large hardwoods, clusters of small oaks, and a few conifers, plus tracts of natural, tall grass; elevation 4900´.

Season & Fees: Open all year; please see Appendix for standard Utah state park entry fees.

Mail & Phone: This is the PlaceState Park, 2601 Sunnyside Avenue, Salt Lake City, UT 84108; ☎(801) 582-1847.

Park Notes: The Mormon culture is deeply involved, totally immersed, in its history. It follows then that Pioneer Trail is the state's most celebrated historic park. The This is the Place Monument which towers above the park and looks westward out across the great valley memorializes the arrival of Brigham Young and the original pioneer party in their promised land. The legendary pronouncement of the remarkable Mormon leader upon reaching the Great Salt Lake Valley in 1847 is generally held to be "This is the place". (History, however, is uncertain of the actual words used by Young. Some historical accounts relate that Young was seriously ill and was being carried on a cart or a stretcher as he and the other 'saints' first glimpsed the valley. One of Young's contemporaries quotes him as saying "Yes, this is the right place; drive on.") The great emigration, which Mormons call "The Gathering" lasted some 20 years and involved more than 70,000 individuals.

▲ Utah 11

STAGECOACH INN
Camp Floyd/Stagecoach Inn State Park

Location: West-central Utah west of Provo.

Access: From Utah State Highway 73 at milepost 20 + .7 in the hamlet of Fairfield (4.8 miles south of the community of Cedar Fort, 20 miles southwest of Lehi), turn east onto 1500 North (a paved local street); proceed 1 block; the inn is on the north side of the street.

Day Use Facilities: Small picnic area just behind (west) of the inn; medium-sized shelter; drinking water; restrooms; medium-sized, streetside parking area.

Overnight Facilities: None; nearest full-service public campground is in Utah Lake State Park.

Activities & Attractions: Renovated, historic inn built in 1858, includes 12 rooms complete with antique furnishings.

Natural Features: Located in Cedar Valley, between the Lake Mountains to the east and the Oquirrh Mountains to the west and north; day use area is on a mown lawn shaded by large hardwoods; elevation 5000´.

Season & Fees: April to October; please see Appendix for standard Utah state park entry fees.

Mail & Phone: Camp Floyd/Stagecoach Inn State Park, 18035 West 1540 North, Fairfield UT 84013; ☎(801) 768-8932.

Park Notes: The inn was built in 1858 by an early settler, John Carson, a Mormon emigrant from Pennsylvania. It was first used as a hotel and an army officers' commissary just before and during the early days of the War Between the States, then as a Pony Express and Overland Stage station. It's hard to imagine that the now tiny, sedate community of Fairfield was, in 1860, the third-largest city in Utah (population

7000, including 4000 civilians and 3000 U.S. Army troops), as a result of the establishment of Camp Floyd (see separate information).

According to historical records, Fairfield became a rip-roaring boomtown, complete with "a riffraff of saloon-keepers (for the 17 saloons), gamblers, women, slickers, thieves and robbers". Carson's little inn "was an oasis of decency in that wild setting". Innkeeper Carson wouldn't even allow "round dances" on the premises, since, in accordance with Mormon precepts, only "square dancing" was permitted. The inn was operated by the Carson family until it was boarded up in 1947. It subsequently was reopened as a state park in 1964. The simple, classic, two-story building is now painted a light gray color, with a matching picket fence which borders the inn and its grounds.

▲ Utah 12

CAMP FLOYD

Camp Floyd/Stagecoach Inn State Park

Location: West-central Utah west of Provo.

Access: From Utah State Highway 73 at milepost 20 + .7 in the hamlet of Fairfield (4.8 miles south of the community of Cedar Fort, 20 miles southwest of Lehi), turn east onto 1500 North (a paved local street); proceed 1 block; the rebuilt camp commissary/park office/information center is on the south side of the street. **Additional Access:** From Highway 73 at milepost 20 + .5 (0.2 mile south of Fairfield), turn southeast onto a paved local road and proceed 0.4 mile; turn south (right) onto an access road for 0.1 mile to the Camp Floyd Cemetery.

Day Use Facilities: None; picnic area and restrooms in the Stagecoach Inn unit; medium-sized parking lot at the cemetery.

Overnight Facilities: None, except that limited camping is permitted during Easter and Memorial Day weekends on a small, grassy flat adjacent to the cemetery; nearest full-service public campground is in Utah Lake State Park.

Activities & Attractions: Site of Camp Floyd, a major, though short-lived, U.S. Army post of the mid-1800's; Camp Floyd Cemetery, completely renovated and landscaped with the cooperation of the American Legion, holds the graves of 84 officers and men of the Army of Utah.

Natural Features: Located on a brushy plain in Cedar Valley; juniper/cedar-dotted mountains flank the valley east and west; elevation 5000´.

Season & Fees: April to October; please see Appendix for standard Utah state park entry fees.

Mail & Phone: Camp Floyd/Stagecoach Inn State Park,18035 West 1540 North, Fairfield UT 84013; ☎(801) 768-8932.

Park Notes: The story of Camp Floyd could have been the basis of a film script for one of those western cavalry epics of the 1940's or 1950's—it happened on that grand of a scale. In June of 1858 an expeditionary force of more than 3000 U.S. troops was sent by President Buchanan to ensure order among the Mormons. Called the "Army of Utah", the brigades set up camp in Fairfield—far enough from Salt Lake City to be more or less inconspicuous, but close enough to carry out the President's orders should a suspected Mormon rebellion arise.

By early November of '58, some 400 log, stone and adobe buildings had been erected on several hundred acres adjoining the south and west edges of Fairfield. During its time, the Army of Utah was the largest single military unit in the United States. The rebellion never fully materialized, and by the end of 1860 most of the troops had been sent elsewhere to contend with an emerging, and far more demanding, conflict. Nearly all of the camp's buildings were razed as the last of the Army of Utah departed in July of 1861.

A key figure throughout all of this was Colonel Philip St. George Cooke, the camp's last commandant, an "impartial friend, humanitarian, soldier, dedicated to the West, unequivocally loyal to the Union....." (Cooke would have been portrayed by John Wayne in the movie version.) Well, you can find out more about Cooke, Camp Floyd, the *Valley Tan* (the local non-Mormon newspaper), and a multitude of other historical details by visiting this outpost yourself. You'll have plenty of good company—Camp Floyd/Stagecoach Inn is a stop for travelers from all over the world.

▲ Utah 13 ♿

UTAH LAKE
State Park

Location: North-central Utah west of Provo.

Access: From Interstate 15 Exit 268 for Center Street in Provo, proceed west on Center Street for 2.6 miles to the park entrance.

Day Use Facilities: Medium-large picnic area; small group picnic area; drinking water; restrooms; large parking lots.

Overnight Facilities: Approximately 30 campsites in somewhat of an open camping arrangement; sites are generally small and closely spaced; parking surfaces are paved, short straight-ins; (it's possible to park a towing vehicle and a trailer side-by-side); ample space for large tents on the lawn; barbecue grills; b-y-o firewood; water at several faucets; restrooms with showers; holding tank disposal station; paved driveways; complete supplies and services are available in Provo.

Activities & Attractions: Swimming area; boating; boat launches and docks; marina; canoeing on the river; fishing for walleye, perch, white bass, catfish; outdoor ice skating rink (December to March); visitor center with meeting/conference rooms; hiking trail; playground.

Natural Features: Located along and near the east shore of Utah Lake and along the banks of the Provo River; the park is landscaped with large, manicured lawns and scattered small to large hardwoods, and trimmed with rail fences; the Wasatch Range rises in clear view a few miles east, the Lake Mountains border the west shore of the lake; elevation 4500´.

Season & Fees: Day use areas open all year; camping permitted March to October;

please see Appendix for standard Utah state park entry and campground fees.

Mail & Phone: Utah Lake State Park, 4400 West Center, Provo, UT 84601; ☎(385) 375-0731 or 375-0733.

Park Notes: It would really be hard to beat this park for looks, since both the local environment and the distant views are very good indeed. If you're planning on picnicking or camping, it might be a good idea to tuck some portable shade in with your beach blanket or tent. Much of the park's lakefront property is allocated to boating activities, but there is still some shoreline left over on Utah's largest freshwater lake for landlubbers.

▲ Utah 14

LOST CREEK
State Park

Location: North-central Utah southeast of Ogden.

Access: From Interstate 84 Exit 111 for Devil's Slide and Croydon (8 miles east of Morgan, 4 miles northwest of Henefer), proceed northeast on a paved local road (past the cement plant) for 1.9 miles to a 'T' intersection at the east edge of the hamlet of Croydon (by the city park); turn north (left) and travel on a winding, paved road for 10.5 miles to the creekside area, on the east (right) side of the road; or continue ahead and up for another 0.5 mile to the top of the dam and the lakeside area.

(Note: if you're westbound on I-84, you could take Exit 115 at Henefer, then, from the north side of the Interstate, proceed northwest on a paved local road for 4.5 miles to Croydon; it'll save about a mile and perhaps a minute. Also note that the access road has been under construction and should be paved all the way to the reservoir by the time you read this; however, if the funds ran out before the paving job was finished, you could have as much as 2 miles of rough, rocky, narrow, sometimes steep and winding, gravel road on the last stretch to the reservoir.)

Day Use Facilities: Vault facility; small parking area adjacent to the dam.

Overnight Facilities: Open camping along the creek, with enough room for approximately a dozen campers.

Activities & Attractions: Boating; paved boat launch; fishing for stocked trout.

Natural Features: Located on the shore of 365-acre Lost Creek Reservoir, and on the banks of Lost Creek below Lost Creek Dam; vegetation consists of scattered, large hardwoods and brush along the creek, mostly grass around the reservoir; bordered by dry, grassy hills and mountains spotted with a few trees; elevation 5800´ to 6000´.

Season & Fees: Open all year, subject to weather conditions; (no fee, subject to change).

Mail & Phone: c/o East Canyon State Park, P.O. Box 97, Morgan, UT 84050; ☎(801) 829-3838.

Park Notes: The road up to the reservoir from Croydon passes through a narrow valley and follows Lost Creek most of the way. The drive along the small stream is pleasant enough to take for its own merits (although the adjacent property is mostly private, agricultural land). (Reportedly, there are no firm plans to develop the park much beyond its basic/primitive state; but a few picnic tables and another vault could spring up at any time.) The reservoir is subject to deep drawdown, so the bottom end of the boat ramp could be several yards from the water's edge by late summer.

▲ Utah 15 ♿

EAST CANYON
State Park

Location: North-central Utah northeast of Salt Lake City.

Access: From Utah State Highway 66 at milepost 1 +.6 (1.6 miles west of the junction of State Highways 66 and 65 south of Henefer, 12 miles southeast of I-84 Exit 103 at Morgan, 10 miles southwest of I-84 Exit 115 at Henefer), turn south onto the park access road and proceed 0.1 mile to the park entrance station; continue ahead past the entrance to the large day use parking areas; or turn east (left) and proceed 0.1 mile to day use and group area parking, or 0.3 mile to the campground.

Day Use Facilities: Medium-sized picnic area; several small ramadas (sun shelters); group picnic/camp area with pavilions (sun shelters), available by reservation only; drinking water; restrooms; several medium-sized and large parking lots.

Overnight Facilities: 31 campsites in the primary camping area, plus additional sites in a parking lot arrangement; (the group picnic/camp area is also available, by reservation only); sites are small to medium-sized, with virtually zero separation; parking pads are gravel, short to medium-length pull-offs or straight-ins; most pads will require some additional leveling; good-sized, but sloped, tent areas; concrete pads for most tables; fire rings and/or barbecue grills; b-y-o firewood; water at several faucets; restrooms; holding tank disposal station; paved driveway; camper supplies at the marina; limited supplies and services are available in Morgan.

Activities & Attractions: Boating; boat launch and docks; marina; fishing for stocked trout; swimming area; (local signs and informational literature state "no beer kegs allowed").

Natural Features: Located on a steep, open hillside above a bay on the north shore of 680-acre East Canyon Reservoir; some trees have been planted, but otherwise most picnic and camp sites are unsheltered; surrounded by the high, brush-and-tree-covered mountains of the Wasatch Range; elevation 5700´.

Season & Fees: Open all year; please see Appendix for reservation information and standard Utah state park entry and campground fees.

Mail & Phone: East Canyon State Park, 5535 South Highway 66, Morgan, UT 84050; ☎(801) 829-6866.

Park Notes: Although it tends to be typically breezy and relatively cool here in summer, some sort of shelter from the bright sunshine would still be a desirable piece of equipment to bring along to this park. The views from this hillside location are quite good. In addition to the main park described here, there are several small, undeveloped park areas at or near the south end of the lake; some of them are vehicle-accessible from Highway 65 via short dirt roads; others are boat-in or walk-in only sites.

 *Utah*

Northeast Mountains

Utah 16 &

ROCKPORT
State Park

Location: North-central Utah north of Heber City.

Access: From Utah State Highway 32 near milepost 23 (5 miles south of Interstate 80 Exit 156 at Wanship, 10 miles north of Kamas, 27 miles north of Heber City), turn east onto the paved park access road and proceed 0.2 mile to the park entrance station, then follow the paved, winding road north for 0.1 mile to 3.5 miles to the camp/picnic areas; the major developed area at Juniper Campground is 3.4 miles from the entrance.

Day Use Facilities: Several small or medium-sized picnic/camp areas with small shelters, vault facilities and parking.

Overnight Facilities: *Juniper Campground:* 35 campsites; sites are small to medium-sized, with minimal to nominal separation; parking pads are paved, medium-length, straight-ins or pull-offs which have been fairly well leveled; most tent areas are medium to large, but somewhat sloped; fire rings and/or barbecue grills; b-y-o firewood; water at several faucets; restrooms with showers, plus auxiliary vault facilities; paved driveways; *additional camping areas:* a number of small to medium-sized, primitive camp areas with vault facilities and limited or no drinking water are available along the park road; (three of these primitive camps are reservable by groups); holding tank disposal station; gas and groceries are available in Wanship, or in Peoa, 5 miles south.

Activities & Attractions: Boating; boat launch and docks, 0.8 mile south of Juniper campground; fishing; small, sandy swimming beach; cross-country ski trail.

Natural Features: Located on hillsides dotted with junipers and sage above the east shore of Rockport Reservoir, a 500-acre impoundment on the Weber River; camp and picnic sites receive minimal to light shade/shelter from hardwoods, junipers and some conifers; surrounded by hills and low mountains; elevation 6100´.

Season & Fees: Main season April to November, plus limited availability in winter; reservations are available for individual campsites in Juniper Campground, and in three group camp areas; please see Appendix for reservation information and standard Utah state park entry and campground fees.

Mail & Phone: Rockport State Park, 9040 North State Highway 302, Rockport, UT 84036; ☎ (435) 336-2241.

Park Notes: Most of the picnic and camp sites have good views of the lake and the surrounding mountains. Juniper is the best-equipped and best-looking of the park's nine camping areas. The other spots have limited water, gravel/dirt driveways and parking areas, and generally less shade/shelter. (Twin Coves Campground, 1.9 miles from the park entrance, also has been somewhat developed and might suit your needs if Juniper is full.)

Utah 17 &

JORDANELLE:
HAILSTONE
State Park

Location: North-central Utah north of Heber City.

Access: From U.S. Highway 40 at Exit 8 (12 miles north of Heber City, 8 miles southeast of Interstate 80 at Silver Crek Junction), turn east onto the park access road and go 0.4 mile to the park.

Day Use Facilities: Several small or medium-sized picnic areas; 40 picnic cabanas; 3 group pavilions; drinking water;

restrooms; several small to large parking lots.

Overnight Facilities: 141 campsites, most with partial hookups; sites are small to medium-sized, with minimal separation; parking pads are paved, medium-length straight-ins or long pull-throughs; most tent areas are medium to large, but a bit sloped; fire rings and barbecue grills; b-y-o firewood; water at several faucets; restrooms with showers; coin-op laundry; holding tank disposal station; paved driveways; complete supplies and services are available in Heber City and Park City.

Activities & Attractions: Sandy swimming beaches; boating; 2 boat launches and docks; fishing; fish cleaning stations; miles of hiking trails; playground; cross-country skiing; large visitor center.

Natural Features: Located on hills along and near the west shore of Jordanelle Reservoir, an impoundment on the Provo River and its tributaries; camp and picnic sites receive zero to light natural shade and shelter from small hardwoods; surrounded by sage slopes, and evergreen-dotted hills; the forested Wasatch Range rises just to the west; elevation 6000´.

Season & Fees: Open all year, with limited services in winter; reservations are available for individual campsites and group camp areas; please see Appendix for reservation information and standard Utah state park entry and campground fees.

Mail & Phone: Jordanelle State Park, P.O. Box 309, Heber City UT 84032; ☎(435) 649-9540.

Park Notes: Near Jordanelle is another, very different state park. Historic Union Pacific Rail Trail State Park is the longest, thinest state park in the Desert Southwest. It consists of the old UP rail bed that's been turned into a hiking, biking, horse and x-c ski trail. The old trackbed runs 28 miles twixt Park City and the shore of Echo Reservoir, passing through the towns of Wanship and Coalville. Most of the route closely (actually *very* closely) parallels Interstate 80, so you and your trailmates are probably not going to gleefully exclaim "Ah, Wilderness!".

▲ **Utah 18** ♿

JORDANELLE:
ROCK CLIFF
State Park

Location: North-central Utah north of Heber City.

Access: From Utah State Highway 32 at milepost 7 +.6 (2.5 miles west of the town of Francis, 7 miles east of the junction of Highway 32 & U.S. Highway 40 north of Heber City), turn north into the park .

Day Use Facilities: Medium-sized picnic area; shelters; group pavilion; drinking water; restrooms; large and small parking areas.

Overnight Facilities: 50 walk-in tent campsites; (a group camp is also available, by reservation); sites are small, with nominal separation; restrooms with showers; camper parking area; gas and groceries are available in Francis.

Activities & Attractions: Nature center; interpretive trails; nature programs; boating and floating; small boat launch; fishing; designated swimming beach.

Natural Features: Located along the banks of the Provo River; camp and picnic sites receive light to medium+ shade/shelter from tall cottonwoods over tall grass or mown grass; bordered by sagey hills, rocky bluffs and hills; elevation 6200´.

Season & Fees: Main season is April to November, plus limited availability in winter; please see Appendix for standard Utah state park entry and campground fees.

Mail & Phone: Jordanelle State Park, P.O. Box 309, Heber City UT 84032; ☎(435) 649-9540.

Park Notes: One of the most scenic trips in the West starts just a couple of miles east of this park unit. The Mirror Lake Highway (Utah 150) begins in Kamas and gently winds up and over the Uinta Mountains to Evanston Wyoming. The scenery is first rate from here to the Utah-Wyo border.

▲ Utah 19 ♿

WASATCH MOUNTAIN
State Park

Location: North-central Utah west of Heber City.

Access: From U.S. Highways 40/189 in midtown Heber City, at the intersection of South Main and 100 South, travel west on Utah State Highway 113 for 3.2 miles to its junction with State Highway 224 in the town of Midway; continue west on Highway 224 (Main Street) for 2 blocks, then go north for another 2 blocks; finally, turn west onto 200 North Street, and follow the highway for 2.2 miles to the park entrance and the visitor center; continue north (right) past the visitor center for 0.4 mile, then turn west (left) to the golf course; or continue past the golf course turnoff for another 0.7 mile to milepost 3 +.3, then turn left into Pine Creek (main) Campground.

Alternate Access: From the junction of U.S. Highway 189 and Utah State Highway 113 in the hamlet of Charleston (23 miles northeast of Provo, 5 miles southwest of Heber City), head north on Highway 113 for 4 miles to Midway and continue as above. (The alternate access would save several miles if you're arriving from Interstate 15 or the Provo metro area.) (Note: Access for the group areas at Little Deer Creek and the Chalet are not listed here since you'll need to check-in at the visitor center first, and you can get detailed directions to them at that time.)

Day Use Facilities: Small picnic area, drinking water, restrooms and parking lot at the visitor center; 2 large pavilions with grills, sinks and electrical outlets (reservable by groups), plus restrooms and a large parking lot are located in the main campground area; group day use is also available at the Chalet (see info below).

Overnight Facilities: *Pine Creek Campground*: 122 individual campsites, including 56 partial-hookup units, and 66 full-hookup units, in 3 loops; sites are standard-issue, state park sized, with good to very good separation; parking pads are paved, medium length straight-ins or medium to long pull-throughs; additional leveling will be required in most sites; tent camping permitted in the Oak Hollow Loop; framed-and-gravelled tent pads; fire rings and barbecue grills in most units; b-y-o firewood; water at sites; restrooms with showers; holding tank disposal station; paved driveways; *Deer Creek Group Camp*: 17 campsites with tent pads, fire rings or barbecue grills, drinking water and restrooms; *Chalet*: ranch-style building with kitchen, banquet tables and restrooms, plus picnic tables and space for rv and tent camping; (Little Deer Creek and Chalet areas are available only to groups, by reservation only); adequate supplies and services are available in Heber.

Activities & Attractions: 36-hole golf course (USGA OK'd) with driving range, (plans call for another 36 holes to be constructed); practice greens and pro shop; visitor center; hiking and equestrian trails; amphitheater for evening programs in the campground; children's fishing pond at the visitor center; orv's permitted in designated areas; in winter, a 7-mile Nordic ski track is established on the golf course; 90 miles of snowmobile trails are maintained within the park and adjacent Uinta National Forest.

Natural Features: Located in Heber Valley on the lower east slopes of the Wasatch Range; vegetation principally consists of varieties of small and large hardwoods, brush and open grassy areas at lower elevations and evergreens at upper levels; high peaks are in view to the north and west, very high peaks rise in the distant south; park area is 22,000 acres; elev. 5500´ to 8700´.

Season & Fees: Open all year, with limited services in winter; please see Appendix for day use and campground reservation information and standard Utah state park entry and campground fees; greens fees $8.00; please contact the park directly for golf course reservations, and for current x-c skiing conditions.

Mail & Phone: Wasatch Mountain State Park, P.O. Box 10, Midway, UT 84049; ☎(435) 654-1791 (visitor center); ☎(435) 654-0532 (golf course).

Park Notes: The park covers a lot of local real estate—most of the west and northwest sections along the edge of Heber Valley and the adjacent foothills and mountains of the Wasatch Range. This is said to be the most popular state park in Utah. In some respects that's surprising since, unlike the busiest parks of many other states, Wasatch Mountain has no major water feature to draw crowds. Several small streams and 10 ponds on the golf course make up most of the open water here. (Although a small portion of state park land lies adjacent to Deer Creek Reservoir, the lake really isn't readily accessible from within the park.) When you take in the mountain views from these slopes, you'll see why campground and group area reservations are recommended well in advance for summer weekends.

▲ Utah 20 ♿

DEER CREEK
State Park

Location: North-central Utah between Provo and Heber City.

Access: From U.S. Highway 189 at milepost 19 +.7 (9 miles southwest of Heber City, 20 miles northeast of Provo), turn northwest onto a paved access road and proceed 0.2 mile to the park entrance; continue beyond the entrance for 0.2 mile, then turn right for 0.1 mile to the campground; or continue ahead for 0.2 mile to the boat launch and parking lot.

Day Use Facilities: Most facilities are shared with the campground; large parking lot.

Overnight Facilities: 33 campsites, including several park 'n walk units; (a group camp area is also available); sites are small to small+, with nil to minimal separation; parking pads are quite long, reasonably level (considering the terrain), paved pull-throughs or straight-ins; some pads may require a little additional leveling; good-sized, fairly level, grassy tent areas; barbecue grills or fire rings; b-y-o firewood; water at several faucets; restrooms with showers; holding tank disposal station; paved driveways; gas and camper supplies along the highway

northeast of the park; adequate supplies and services are available in Heber City.

Activities & Attractions: Boating; sailing; windsurfing; boat launch; fishing for stocked trout, also largemouth bass, walleye, perch and crayfish; evening campfire programs in summer.

Natural Features: Located on a steep, open slope on the south shore of Deer Creek Reservoir, an impoundment on the Provo River at the head of Provo Canyon in the southwest corner of Heber Valley; park vegetation consists of sections of mown lawns planted with hardwoods and conifers; the reservoir is bordered by high mountains with grassy/brushy lower slopes and partially timbered tops; typically windy; elevation 5400´.

Season & Fees: April to November; please see Appendix for reservation information and standard Utah state park entry and campground fees.

Mail & Phone: Deer Creek State Park, P.O. Box 257, Midway, UT 84049; ☎(435) 654-0171.

Park Notes: Views of the Wasatch Range and of the reservoir from the park area are very striking. For really great views, spend some time along the east shore. The lofty, rugged peaks of The Wasatch, and the deep blue lake speckled with the brilliantly colored sails of sailboats or windsurfers supply a vivid image. Stiff winds funnel easterly through Provo Canyon and spill down off the mountains to provide a predictably good sailing environment. If you're not up to windsurfing, some simple fun can be had angling for crayfish. All you need is a small hunk of meat tried to a string, then dunk it into rocky or weedy water that's 3-5 feet deep. (Since you don't even need a hook, maybe the sport should be called 'dangling'.) The reservoir has been the object of an intensive cleanup program because of problems resulting from local agricultural practices and recreational use. (Treated household water from here is piped to nearly a million people annually. One of the catch-phrases of the campaign states "You never know when *you* might be drinking a glass of water from Deer Creek Reservoir".)

▲ **Utah 21**

SCOFIELD:
MADSEN BAY
State Park

Location: Central Utah northwest of Price.

Access: From Utah State Highway 96 at milepost 13 +.9 (9 miles southwest of the junction of Highway 96 and U.S. Highway 6 near Colton, 7.5 miles north of the community of Scofield), turn west onto a paved access road and proceed 0.1 mile to the small North Shore area; or continue around the north end of the lake and then southwest along the west shore for an additional mile to the Lakeside section; or continue westerly on gravel/dirt for a final 0.3 mile to the Upper Pavilion area.

Day Use Facilities: Small picnic/camp area and vault facilities at the North Shore area; small picnic/camp area, group shelter and restrooms at the Lakeside area; small picnic/camp area, group shelter, and vault facilities at the Upper Pavilion area.

Overnight Facilities: Approximately 25 campsites in the 3 areas listed in the Day Use section above; sites vary from small to large, with straight-in or random parking arrangements; ample space for medium to large tents in about half of the sites; water at central faucets; vault facilities or restrooms as listed above; gas and camper supplies are available in Scofield.

Activities & Attractions: Boating; boat launch at the Lakeside area; trout fishing.

Natural Features: Located on or above the north/northwest shore of 2800-acre Scofield Reservoir, an impoundment on the Price River in the mountains on the Wasatch Plateau; North Shore and Lakeside sites are generally unsheltered; Upper Pavilion sites are forested; elevation 7600´.

Season & Fees: Main season April to November, available at other times for limited/winter activities; please see Appendix for standard Utah state park entry and campground fees.

Mail & Phone: Scofield State Park, P.O. Box 166, Price, UT 84501; ☎(435) 448-9449 (summer); ☎(435) 637-8497 (winter).

Park Notes: Of the trio of small areas at this end of the reservoir, the Upper Pavilion area, which is tucked away in a forested pocket, gets the nod for having the nicest setting. Madsen Bay is said to be a popular spot for group picnics and family reunions.

▲ **Utah 22** ♿

SCOFIELD:
MOUNTAIN VIEW
State Park

Location: Central Utah northwest of Price.

Access: From Utah State Highway 96 at milepost 12 +.2 (10.5 miles southwest of the junction of Highway 96 and U.S. Highway 6 near Colton, 0.7 mile north of the Scofield Dam, 6 miles north of the community of Scofield), turn west onto the paved park access road and proceed 0.2 mile (the roadway makes a left-handed '180') to the park entrance station; continue ahead, then swing right to the campground and the picnic area.

Day Use Facilities: Small picnic area; drinking water; vault facilities; medium-sized parking lots.

Overnight Facilities: 35 campsites in 5 rows in a tiered arrangement; sites are very small, with nil separation; most parking pads are gravel, short straight-ins; most pads will require a little additional leveling (although they're reasonably level, considering the slope); adequate space for small to medium-sized tents; barbecue grills; b-y-o firewood; water at several faucets; restrooms with showers; holding tank disposal station; paved driveways; gas and camper supplies are available in Scofield.

Activities & Attractions: Boating; boat launch and docks; trout fishing.

Natural Features: Located above the east/northeast shore of 2800-acre Scofield Reservoir, on the east slope of the mountainous Wasatch Plateau; camp and picnic sites are minimally to lightly shaded by hardwoods and a few conifers; the mountains are mostly sage-covered, with large stands of aspens and conifers; elevation 7600´.

Season & Fees: Main season April to November; available at other times for limited winter activities; campsite reservations accepted; please see Appendix for reservation information and standard Utah state park entry and campground fees.

Mail & Phone: Scofield State Park, P.O. Box 166, Price, UT 84501; ☎(435) 448-9449 (summer); ☎(435) 637-8497 (winter).

Park Notes: Most of the lake and its attendant mountains are in full view from this elevated spot. If you're camping, you might want to try for a site a little farther down the slope. The view might not be quite as grand as that from the upper rows, but the site will be a bit more removed from the surprisingly busy highway which passes within a few yards of the higher camp units. The high mountain country you'll see across the lake is a small portion of what is one of the most scenic regions in Utah. You might like to consider arriving or departing Scofield Park via Highways 264 and 31, to or from U.S. Highway 89 in Fairview. (A glance at a highway map will show you the route.) The roads pass up and over the 9000´ level, and some of the plateau's peaks top that mark by 2000´. The grade is very steep and the road is very twisty (especially on Highway 264 on the east slope of the plateau); but once you're up near Skyline Drive the road levels-out and passes through a conifer forest interspersed with sub-alpine prairie. A good way to begin or end a trip.

🌲 **Utah 23** ♿

STARVATION
State Park

Location: Northeast Utah between Vernal and Heber City.

Access: From U.S. Highway 40 at milepost 87 +.2 (on the west edge of Duchesne, 58 miles west of Vernal, 68 miles east of Heber City), turn north onto a paved access road and proceed 3.5 miles to the park entrance station; just past the entrance, turn right, and continue for 0.1 mile to the main park area.

Day Use Facilities: Medium-sized picnic area; group picnic/ camp area (available by reservation only); large parking lot.

Overnight Facilities: 31 campsites; (a group camp/picnic area is also available, by reservation); sites are small, level, with limited separation provided by wooden-walled windbreaks; parking surfaces are paved, medium to long pull-throughs or straight-ins; large, framed tent pads in some sites; barbecue grills; firewood is usually for sale, or b-y-o; water at several faucets; restrooms with showers; holding tank disposal station; paved driveways; limited supplies and services are available in Duchesne.

Activities & Attractions: Boating; boat launch and dock; fishing for trout, bass and walleye; small playground.

Natural Features: Located along the shore (day use area) and on an open bluff (campground) overlooking 3000-acre Starvation Lake (Reservoir), a dry-rimmed impoundment on the Strawberry River; campground vegetation consists of patches of watered and mown grass and a few small hardwoods and evergreens; a very large, grassy field lies behind the camping area; the lofty Uinta Mountains are visible to the north; windy; elevation 5700´.

Season & Fees: Open all year; please see Appendix for reservation information and standard Utah state park entry and campground fees.

Mail & Phone: Starvation State Park, P.O. Box 584, Duchesne, UT 84021; ☎(435) 738-2326.

Park Notes: For a semi-arid location such as this, there are some surprisingly good views from 'up on top', in the camping area—colorful hills, rimrocks, and the High Uintas (snow-capped much of the year) way off in the distance.

▲ Utah 24

STEINAKER
State Park

Location: Northeast Utah north of Vernal.

Access: From U.S. Highway 191 at milepost 206 + .4 (at the northeast corner of Steinaker Lake, 5.5 miles north of midtown Vernal, 35 miles south of the junction of U.S. 191 and Utah State Highway 44 at Flaming Gorge), turn west onto the paved park access road and proceed 1.6 miles to the park.

Day Use Facilities: Small picnic area; 2 group pavilions (sun shelters); small parking area.

Overnight Facilities: 31 campsites; sites are about average in size, with nominal separation; most parking pads are paved, long pull-throughs, plus a few medium-length straight-ins; additional leveling may be required in some sites; adequate space for small to medium-sized tents in most sites; some units have framed tent pads; fire rings and barbecue grills; b-y-o firewood; water at several faucets; restrooms; holding tank disposal station; paved driveways; adequate+ supplies and services are available in Vernal.

Activities & Attractions: Boating; boat launch; fishing for trout, bass and bluegill; waterskiing; sandy swimming beach.

Natural Features: Located along a small bay on the west shore of 750-acre Steinaker Lake; park vegetation consists of medium-height hardwoods, and junipers, on a grass-and-sage slope; the local area is encircled by barren or juniper-dotted bluffs and hills; partially forested ridges and low mountains are visible in the distance; maximum depth of the lake is about 125 feet; elevation 5500´.

Season & Fees: Open all year; please see Appendix for reservation information and standard Utah state park entry and campground fees.

Mail & Phone: Steinaker State Park, Steinaker Lake North 4335, Vernal, UT 84078; ☎(435) 789-4432.

Park Notes: Almost all of the activities here are water-oriented, so about three-fourths of the park's annual visitors come in June, July and August. By late July, the water temperature climbs into the low 70's, making the lake a good spot to cool off in this barren territory's midsummer sizzle. With only eight inches of annual rain and snow, the surroundings are a mite on the dry side; still, the lake's tree-lined shore stands in congenial opposition to the park's rocky surroundings. Autumn's colors show the place at its best.

▲ Utah 25

RED FLEET
State Park

Location: Northeast Utah north of Vernal.

Access: From U.S. Highway 191 at a point 10 miles north of Vernal and 26 miles south of the junction of U.S. 191 and Utah State Highway 44 near Flaming Gorge, turn east onto a park access road and proceed 2 miles to the park.

Day Use Facilities: Medium-sized picnic area; small ramadas (sun shelters); drinking water; restrooms; parking near sites and in a medium-sized parking lot.

Overnight Facilities: 29 campsites; sites are small, essentially level, with nil separation for parking slots, minimal to nominal separation for table areas (see Notes below); parking surfaces are short+ straight-ins; adequate space for medium to large tents; small ramadas (sun shelters); barbecue grills and/or fire rings; b-y-o firewood; water at several faucets; restrooms; holding tank disposal station; adequate+ supplies and services are available in Vernal.

Activities & Attractions: Boating; boat launch; fishing; designated swimming beach; dinosaur footprints.

Natural Features: Located on a bluff overlooking the south-west shore of Red Fleet Reservoir, an impoundment on Big Brush Creek; area vegetation consists mostly of sparse grass, low brush and junipers/cedars; the lake is bordered by multi-colored bluffs and low hills sparingly dotted with junipers; the Uinta Mountains rise above 12,000´ in the not-too-distant northwest; typically breezy; elevation 5500´.

Season & Fees: April to November; please see Appendix for reservation information and standard Utah state park entry and campground fees.

Mail & Phone: c/o Steinaker State Park, Steinaker Lake North 4335, Vernal, UT 84078; ☎(435) 789-4432.

Park Notes: Red Fleet gets its name from a red sandstone formation at the north shore of the reservoir which fancifully resembles a rocky armada sailing across the hills and rolling high desert plains of this region. Most of the picnic sites are near the edge of the bluff and enjoy a good view. The campsites are in a somewhat unorthodox arrangement: the parking slots are angled off of the main driveway and are fender-to-fender; the camp tables and ramadas are walk-ins, and most are in a large, central cluster in an 'infield' bordered by the parking spaces; a few tables are in the 'outfield'. The hundreds of dinosaur tracks found in the hardened mud and sand here are those of three-toed, two-legged critters (*tridactyl bipeds*) of unknown species. Generally speaking, the 200-million-year-old footprints are best viewed in early morning or late afternoon on a sunny day. The shadows cast by the low sun angle make the prints easier to distinguish from the surrounding surface.

▲ Utah 26

UTAH FIELD HOUSE OF NATURAL HISTORY
State Park

Location: Northeast Utah in Vernal.

Access: From U.S. Highway 40 (East Main Street) in midtown Vernal, (near milepost 146 in the 200 block, 0.2 mile east of the big intersection at the junction of U.S. 40 and U.S. 191), the park is on the north side of Main Street.

Day Use Facilities: None (there's a picnic area in a city park behind the state park); drinking water and restrooms inside the building; medium-sized parking lot; additional streetside parking is available.

Overnight Facilities: None; nearest public campground is in Steinaker State Park.

Activities & Attractions: Museum with exhibits of geology, paleontology and history of the Uinta Mountain and Basin region, including fossils, fluorescent minerals, plus murals and paintings depicting prehistoric and contemporary scenes; dinosaur garden features more than a dozen life-size models of prehistoric animals in a natural setting; science reference library and classroom; educational and interpretive programs, mostly in summer.

Natural Features: Located in-town surrounded by high desert plains, hills and mountains; elevation 5300´.

Season & Fees: Open all year; please see Appendix for standard Utah state park entry fees.

Mail & Phone: Utah Field House of Natural History, 235 East Main Street, Vernal, UT 84078; ☎(435) 789-3799.

Park Notes: The museum presents a wealth of information, but there's a good possibility that you and your road partners will spend more time outside in the dino garden (especially if they're kids). The life-size, life-like models are portrayed in authentic surroundings. Most of the 'regulars' from aeons past are present and accounted-for, including brontosaurus, triceratops, and of course, tyrannosaurus rex. A few of them aren't quite as familiar. One of the more unusual breeds is stegosaurus, a five-ton, four-legged, fork-tailed monster with a dozen large, spearhead-shaped plates pointing skyward from along both sides of its backbone. Trying to keep all of these parts going in the same direction is a tiny head with a brain the size of a rat's. (One visitor nicknamed it "Politician".) The garden includes trees and shrubs trimmed to look like foliage from the Age of Giants, and there's a pond and a swamp to complete the picture. Paved paths let you walk among these leviathans, and the displays are lit in the evening.

Utah ⚕

Southwest High Desert

🏔 Utah 27 ♿

YUBA
State Park

Location: Central Utah between Nephi and Fillmore.

Access: From Interstate 15 (southbound) Exit 202 for Yuba Lake (21 miles southwest of Nephi, 35 miles northwest of Fillmore), proceed to the east side of the Interstate, then travel south/southwest on a paved local road for 4.2 miles; turn east (left) into the park entrance. **Alternate Access:** From Interstate 15 (northbound) Exit 188 for Scipio (22 miles northeast of Fillmore), cross over to the west side of the freeway, then head north/northeast on a frontage road for 3.9 miles; turn east (right) and pass under the Interstate and continue northeast for another 6.3 miles to the park.

Day Use Facilities: Small picnic area; medium-sized, group ramada (sun shelter); drinking water; restrooms; medium-sized parking lot.

Overnight Facilities: *Oasis Campground*: 19 campsites; (a group camping area with a pair of small sun ramadas is also available); sites are medium sized, with minimal to fair separation; parking pads are paved, mostly long pull-throughs, plus a few medium to long straight-ins; a little to a lot of additional leveling will be required in most sites; ample space for large tents on framed-and-gravelled tent pads; ramadas (arched, sun/wind shelters) for all sites; barbecue grills and fire rings; b-y-o firewood; water at several faucets; restrooms with showers; holding tank disposal station; paved driveways; gas and groceries are available in Scipio.

Activities & Attractions: Boating; boat launch; fishing for northern pike, channel cat, walleye and perch; swimming area; designated orv area nearby.

Natural Features: Located on a slope on the northwest shore of Yuba Lake (originally named Sevier Bridge Reservoir); the reservoir is a 22-mile-long, 10,000-acre impoundment on the Sevier River, constructed as a source of water for irrigation and industrial use; picnic and camp sites are minimally to lightly shaded by small and large hardwoods on a surface of mostly sparse, natural grass and sage and other short brush; a section of watered and mown grass decorates the camp loop's infield; a long line of hills forms the western backdrop of the park; high and dry, timber-topped mountains lie east and south across the lake; elevation 5000´.

Season & Fees: Open all year; campsite reservations accepted; please see Appendix for reservation information and standard Utah state park entry and campground fees.

Mail & Phone: Yuba State Park, P.O. Box 88, Levan, UT 84639; ☎(435) 758-2611.

Park Notes: Most picnic and camp sites have a good lake view, particularly those in the group camp area—they're perched higher up on the slope and have an unrestricted view in most directions. The individual picnic sites are tiny and closely spaced, but most of the standard camp spots are good-sized—and some of the pull-through parking pads could accommodate a circus train. Although the Interstate is only a mile or so to the west, you'd never know it if you hadn't just exited from the four-lane. The line of hills behind the park forms a very effective visual and acoustical barrier which nicely isolates this freeway-convenient spot. The park's Painted Rocks unit, on the east side of the lake, is accessible off the west side of Utah State Highway 28 at a point midway between Levan and Gunnison. Painted Rocks has primitive picnicking and camping, vault facilities and a boat ramp.

🏔 Utah 28 ♿

PALISADE
State Park

Location: Central Utah south of Manti.

Access: From U.S. Highway 89 at milepost 217 (at the northern edge of the town of Sterling, 5 miles south of Manti), turn east onto a paved access road; travel east and north for 1.7 miles, then turn northwest (left) into the park entrance; the Sanpitch camp area is just to the left of the entrance; or turn right and proceed 0.1 mile to 0.6 mile to the day use area, East camp area and the Arapien camp loop.

Day Use Facilities: Small picnic area; medium-sized pavilion (sun shelter) reservable by groups; small parking lot.

Overnight Facilities: 53 campsites in 2 strings and a loop; (a group camp area is also available); sites are small to medium-sized, with nil to nominal separation; parking pads are paved, mostly level, medium to long straight-ins or pull-throughs; excellent tenting opportunities in many sites, especially in the Arapien loop; b-y-o barbecue grill and fuel is recommended; water at numerous faucets; restrooms with showers; auxiliary vault facilities; holding tank disposal station; paved driveways; gas and groceries in Sterling; adequate supplies and services are available in Manti.

Activities & Attractions: Boating (motorless); fishing; swimming beach; 9-hole golf course with pro shop; x-c skiing; ice fishing; nearby historic town of Manti hosts an impressive pageant each summer.

Natural Features: Located along the north and east shores of 70-acre Palisade Lake (Reservoir); mown and watered lawns throughout most of the park; hardwoods, conifers and bushes provide limited shade/shelter for picnic and camp sites; some campsites have small plots of lawn between sites; picnic sites and many campsites are lakeside; the lake is surrounded by low, dry, juniper-dotted hills; elevation 5900´.

Season & Fees: Main park season is April to November, plus limited availability for winter activities; greens fees $7.00; please see Appendix for reservation information and standard Utah state park entry and campground fees.

Mail & Phone: Palisade State Park, P.O. Box H, Manti, UT 84642; ☎(435) 835-7275 (office); ☎(435) 835-4653 (golf course).

Park Notes: This has been a very popular recreation area since 1873, when a neighborhood go-getter named Daniel Funk, with a little help from Brigham Young, wheeled and dealt with the local Sanpitch Indians for the deed to some land in this small valley. From the onset of the project, Funk and Young are said to have foreseen the need for a recreation spot to serve the area's growing population. Before long, a dam was built and the water of Sixmile Creek was diverted to flood the valley to a depth of about 20 feet. Originally called Funk's Lake, it became a popular resort, complete with a dance hall and a small steamboat for lake 'cruises'. Well, the dance hall is gone and the steamboat no longer plies the lake's placid waters, but the park's landscaping has been improved a lot in modern times. If you're interested in camping here, get a campsite res in early—many of the favorite lakeside sites are booked months in advance. Don't be too discouraged, though, if you're an outsider, since they usually set aside some non-reservable sites for drop-ins.

▲ Utah 29

TERRITORIAL STATEHOUSE
State Park

Location: Central Utah in Fillmore.

Access: From Interstate 15 (southbound) Exit 167 for Business Route I-15 (at the north end of Fillmore), proceed south on Business 15 through the center of town for 1.7 miles to a point just south of midtown; turn west (right) onto the first driveway south of the county courthouse and proceed 100 yards to the small state park parking lot on the west side of the Statehouse. **Alternate Access:** Interstate 15 (northbound) Exit 163 for Business Route I-15 (at the south end of Fillmore), travel north on Biz 15 for 2.2 miles; turn left into the driveway and continue as above. (Note: additional, streetside parking is available along First South, just south of the park.)

Day Use Facilities: Small picnic area; drinking water and restrooms inside the Statehouse; small parking lot.

Overnight Facilities: None; nearest public campgrounds (Fishlake National Forest) are on the Chalk Creek Road, 6 miles southeast of midtown Fillmore.

Activities & Attractions: Utah's oldest existing government building serves as a three-floor museum which houses a fine collection of late nineteenth and early twentieth century furnishings, artifacts and examples of pioneer lifestyles; also, the interior of an 1867 schoolhouse at the southwest corner of the park grounds, is available for viewing upon request; a relocated log cabin houses the Millard hearse.

Natural Features: Located in Pahvant Valley just west of the forested Pahvant Range; the park is landscaped with large sections of mown lawns and paved walks well trimmed with flowers and shrubs and lightly to moderately shaded by large hardwoods; elevation 5100´.

Season & Fees: Open all year; please see Appendix for standard Utah state park entry fees.

Mail & Phone: Territorial Statehouse State Park, P.O. Box 657, Fillmore, UT 84631; ☎(435) 743-5316.

Park Notes: There are perhaps three-dozen really first-rate historical state park museums in the West. In the Desert Southwest, Territorial Statehouse is equalled or surpassed by only one or two others—it's *that* good. The present building is actually only the south wing of the Statehouse which was commissioned by Brigham Young to be built in anticipation of Utah's statehood.

Young had chosen Fillmore as the new state capitol because of its central location.) The original architect's plans called for a red sandstone structure with four wings joined to a rotunda topped by a Moorish dome. But the Territorial Legislature met for only one full session in the partially completed capitol complex before the seat of government was moved back to Salt Lake City.

The orphaned wing eventually fell into a state of disrepair, but it was renovated in 1930 and reopened as a museum. Each room on the main floor is arranged to depict a room in what could be called an early 'model' home: kitchen, dining room, parlor, bedroom, etc. The main hallway is lined with glass display cases containing scores of small items and documents. Upstairs is the sizeable legislative hall with its arched ceiling, polished hardwood floors, and orderly rows of wooden chairs—all bordered by well-windowed walls lined with a collection of antique pianos. Everything in this place is mint.

▲ Utah 30 ♿

FREMONT INDIAN
State Park

Location: Central Utah southwest of Richfield.

Access: From Interstate 70 Exit 17 for Fremont Indian Museum (17 miles east of the junction of Interstates 70 & 15 near Cove Fort, 5 miles west of Sevier), proceed to the north side of the Interstate, then travel east (right) on a paved road which parallels the Interstate for 0.4 mile to a 'T' intersection; bear right, and continue for an additional 0.8 mile; turn north (left) into the visitor center parking lot. **Additional Access** for Castle Rock Campground, (established within Fishlake National Forest, operated by the state park): from the south side of I-70 Exit 17, proceed west/southwest on a gravel access road for 1 mile to the campground.

Day Use Facilities: Small picnic area; drinking water and restrooms inside the visitor center; large parking lot.

Overnight Facilities: 31 campsites; sites are small+, with nominal separation; parking pads are gravel, mostly medium-length straight-ins plus a few pull-throughs; adequate space for medium to large tents in some sites; water at a central faucet; restrooms; gravel driveway; gas and camper supplies in Joseph, 9 miles northeast.

Activities & Attractions: Visitor center featuring an orientation video and comprehensive displays depicting the history and culture of the Fremont Indians; 3 interpretive trails, including a paved, handicapped access trail to Indian rock art, a second trail with exhibits about how the Indians imaginatively used the resources of their environment, and a third trail to a canyon overlook; guided tours by appointment; trout fishing in Clear Creek.

Natural Features: Located in Clear Creek Canyon in the Pahvant Range; the visitor center, trails and rock art are in Little Dog Canyon, a small side canyon on the north side of the main canyon; campsites receive light to medium shade from large hardwoods and junipers; bordered by pine and juniper-covered hills and mountains; total park area is 1000 acres; elevation 5900´.

Season & Fees: Open all year; please see Appendix for standard Utah state park entry and campground fees.

Mail & Phone: Fremont Indian State Park, 11550 West Clear Creek Canyon Road, Sevier, UT 84766; ☎(435) 527-4631.

Park Notes: The Fremont Indians are an anthropological mystery—nothing is known of their origin, or the reason(s) for their disappearance about 800 years ago. But they were unique enough in their own primitive way of life to merit a separate niche in the scientific world. The largest Fremont village discovered to date is the one in Clear Creek Canyon. This village, which contained more than 100 structures, was uncovered on a hill known as Five Finger Knoll in 1983. Fourteen months of painstaking digging by archaeologists produced about seven tons of potentially valuable material. (Shortly after the dig was done, the hill was leveled to make room for the new stretch of Interstate 70 which you'll use to reach the park.)

One of the principal attractions here is the plentiful Indian rock art, and it draws the question: do the etchings tell ancient tales, or depict deep religious beliefs, or are they merely stone age doodles or primeval graffiti? (At least one of the scratchings looks like a twelfth century version of the twentieth century scribbling "Kilroy was here".) If you can't take the time to take the trails, even a brief stop at the impressive visitor center is worth breaking your cruise-controlled Interstate stride for. The displays are of high quality—some of the best of their kind in the Southwest.

▲ **Utah 31**

MINERSVILLE
State Park

Location: Southwest Utah west of Beaver.

Access: From Utah State Highway 121 at milepost 96 +.8 (11 miles west of Beaver, 8 miles east of Minersville), turn northwest onto a paved park access road and proceed 0.3 mile to the park.

Day Use Facilities: Medium-sized picnic area; drinking water; restrooms; medium-sized parking lot (plus overflow parking).

Overnight Facilities: 29 campsites with electrical hookups in 3 rows; sites are small, level, with nil separation; parking pads are packed gravel, medium-length pull-throughs or very short straight-ins; tent space varies from very small to large; small ramadas (sun/wind shelters) for all sites; barbecue grills; b-y-o firewood; water at faucets throughout; restrooms with showers; holding tank disposal station; paved driveways; gas and groceries in Minersville; limited+ supplies and services are available in Beaver.

Activities & Attractions: Boating; boat launch and docks; fishing for stocked rainbow and cutthroat trout.

Natural Features: Located on the southeast shore of 1100-acre Minersville Reservoir; picnic sites are shadeless or very lightly shaded; campsites receive minimal to light natural shade from large hardwoods; surrounded by rolling sage plains and dryish, partly forested hills and mountains; park area is 207 acres; elevation 5600´.

Season & Fees: April to November; campsite reservations accepted; please see Appendix for reservation information and standard Utah state park entry and campground fees.

Mail & Phone: Minersville State Park, P.O. Box 51, Beaver, UT 84713; ☎(435) 438-5472.

Park Notes: Minersville's principal drawing cards are fishing, and to some extent, boating. About one hundred thousand trout are planted annually; most of the angling action is seen March through June. It's possible to come up with some good catches even if you're boatless, since shore fishing is said to be reasonably productive. The park is just across the narrow, long lake from the dam, so the reservoir's deepest water is not too far offshore.

Minersville "never fills up", so you can probably count on having a peak-weekend picnic or camp site here when other park and forest areas are full. (If you motor to Minersville via Interstate 15, as most visitors do, you'll notice that the burg of Beaver has two freeway exits, one at either end of town, as a number of small Interstate communities do. Thus you'll need to take a slow, and potentially fuel-wasting, two-mile tour of Beaver's business district. As you head west toward Minersville on Utah 21 and pass under the Interstate, take a look around: is there any reason (other than a commercial one) why they couldn't have constructed just a single Beaver exit here? Ed.)

▲ Utah 32 ♿

IRON MISSION
State Park

Location: Southwest Utah in Cedar City.

Access: From Utah State Highway 130 (North Main Street/ Business Route I-15) at milepost 3 in Cedar City (0.8 mile north of the junction of State Highways 130 & 14 at midtown Cedar City, 2.2 miles south of Interstate 15 Exit 62 at the north edge of Cedar City) turn west into the park parking lot. (Note that you can get here from Interstate 15 by taking any of the 3 exits for Cedar City—57, 59, or 62—but probably the best bets are Exit 59 if northbound, then east for a mile into midtown, then north on Utah 130 for 0.8 mile; or Exit 62 if southbound, then south on Utah 130 for 2.2 miles.)

Day Use Facilities: Drinking water; restrooms; small and large parking lots; (picnic area in a city park, on North Main 0.2 mile south of the state park).

Overnight Facilities: None; nearest public campground is Cedar Canyon (Dixie National Forest) on State Highway 14, 12 miles southeast of Cedar City.

Activities & Attractions: Collection of horse-drawn vehicles, including a milk wagon, sleigh, hearse, farm equipment, Wells Fargo stagecoach replica, carriages, and a bullet-riddled Concord stagecoach from the Four Corners region (Butch Cassidy's old stomping grounds); a diorama depicts the original ironworks; collection of some 200 Indian artifacts used by Southern Paiutes; examples of quiltwork and other pioneer crafts; the grounds and sheds behind the main building contain a conglomeration of hundreds of wheels from assorted old conveyances and implements.

Natural Features: Located on nicely landscaped grounds in Cedar Valley; the main building is bordered by large sections of mown lawns dotted with a few trees, trimmed by a rail fence;
the mountains of the Markagunt Plateau rise above 11,000´ to the east; elevation 5800´.

Season & Fees: Open all year; please see Appendix for standard Utah state park entry fees.

Mail & Phone: Iron Mission State Park, 585 North Main, P.O. Box 1079, Cedar City, UT 84720; ☎ (435) 586-9290.

Park Notes: Self-sufficiency was of major importance to the early Utah Mormons, and one crucial component which they were short of was iron for fabricating industrial, agricultural and domestic implements. After iron was discovered near present-day Cedar City in the early 1850's, Brigham Young sent a band of volunteers on a mission to mine the strategic material and to produce a crude, but useable, form of ferrous metal. The workers of the so-called "Iron Mission", using a home-built blast furnace, turned-out their first ironware about ten months into the project. After six years of success, periodically interrupted by floods, freezes, famines, furnace failures and Indian uprisings, the group was finally disbanded.

Nowadays, there's certainly enough oxidized metal on the park's premises to lead you to think that just *maybe* one of the old wagon wheel hoops or plowshares or dish pans decorating the grounds or stored in the shed out back was made from raw material produced by the original crew of the Iron Mission. Some iron of slightly more recent vintage is also on display. Among the assemblage of vehicles from horse-and-buggy days is a unique Studebaker White Top Wagon, an ancestor of the station wagon that was powered by a hayburner instead of a V8. The commodious White Top is said to have been a favorite of large Mormon families. Riding with the big Stude, like Sancho alongside Don Quixote, is a compact Stanhope Phaeton. (There may be a collection of pork barrels somewhere around here too. Ed.)

🌲 **Utah 33**

GUNLOCK
State Park

Location: Southwest Utah northwest of St. George.

Access: From Utah State Highway 18 at milepost 3 +.2 (2 miles north of St. George) turn northwest onto Sunset Boulevard and travel 12 miles (through Santa Clara) to a 3-way junction; turn north (right) onto another local paved road (should be signed for "Gunlock" and "Gunlock Reservoir") and proceed 5.9 miles; turn west (left) onto a paved park access road and proceed 0.25 mile to the parking lot and boat launch. **Alternate Access:** From Utah State Highway 18 at milepost 20 +.2 in the community of Veyo (19 miles north of St. George, 6 miles southwest of Central), turn southwest onto Center Street and head out of town on a paved, (sometimes steep and winding) local road for 7 miles to the hamlet of Gunlock; continue through Gunlock and south for another 2.4 miles; turn west (right) onto the parking lot access road and continue as above.

Day Use Facilities: Vault facilities; large parking lot.

Overnight Facilities: None; nearest public campground is in Snow Canyon State Park.

Activities & Attractions: Boating; boat launch and dock; fishing for bass and catfish.

Natural Features: Located in a valley east of the Beaver Dam Mountains on the east shore of Gunlock Reservoir, a 240-acre impoundment on the Santa Clara River; shoreline vegetation consists mostly of scattered hardwoods and brush; bordered by sage-and-juniper-covered hills and mountains; elevation 3400´.

Season & Fees: Open all year; (no fee).

Mail & Phone: c/o Snow Canyon State Park, P.O. Box 140, Santa Clara, UT 84738; ☎(435) 628-2255.

Park Notes: There's a nice little place on a small, treeless point a few tenths of a mile north of the parking lot where you can sit near the water's edge and enjoy the surrounding scenery—the small, blue lake in a narrow valley bordered by red-and-biege hills and distant mountains. This could be a good park someday. It is suggested that you periodically check with the state parks department to determine if the planned "campground, marina, and golf course" have been built yet.

🌲 **Utah 34 ♿**

SNOW CANYON
State Park

Location: Southwest Utah north of St. George.

Access: From Utah State Highway 18 at milepost 11 +.3 (9 miles north of St. George, 9 miles south of Veyo), turn west onto State Highway 300; proceed west then south for 1.5 miles to the Galoot day use (and primitive camping) area on the east (left) side of the road; or continue southerly for another 0.8 mile, then turn east (left) into Shivwits Campground and day use area.

Day Use Facilities: Small individual and group picnic areas at Galoot and Shivwits; (group areas are available by reservation); ramadas (sun shelters) in both areas; drinking water and vault facilities at Galoot;

drinking water and restrooms nearby at Shivwits; small parking areas.

Overnight Facilities: 31 campsites, including 14 with partial hookups; (a few sites can accommodate small groups); sites in the hookup section are small, with minimal separation; parking pads are paved, level, short to medium-length, parallel pull-throughs; hookup loop does not readily accommodate tents; small ramadas (sun shelters) for hookup sites; sites in the standard loop are small to medium-sized, with nominal to fairly good separation; parking pads are gravel, level, short to medium-length straight-ins; some fairly nice tent sites in the standard loop; fireplaces; firewood is often for sale, or b-y-o; water at several faucets; restrooms with showers; holding tank disposal station; paved driveways; complete supplies and services are available in St. George.

Activities & Attractions: Trails to nearby volcanic cinder cones, lava caves, pictographs, sand dunes, overlook points and Johnson Arch, plus 3.5-mile (each-way) West Canyon hiking trail; nature trail; sandstone cliffs and hills behind the campground are said to be "great for climbing" and "a favorite of rappelers" (if you know the ropes).

Natural Features: Located within 3-mile-long Snow Canyon and in the hills north of and above the canyon; canyon walls are swirled red rock and sage-covered slopes; picnic areas are minimally to lightly shaded by hardwoods; campground vegetation consists of some mown grass, natural grass, tall poplars and a few other scattered hardwoods and bushes; park area is 65,000 acres; elevation 2600´ to 3500´.

Season & Fees: Open all year; campsite reservations accepted; please see Appendix for reservation information and standard Utah state park entry and campground fees.

Mail & Phone: Snow Canyon State Park, P.O. Box 140, Santa Clara, UT 84738; ☎(435) 628-2255.

Park Notes: Before you leave Highway 18, you can get a bird's eye view of Snow Canyon by taking the gravel road west of the highway near mile 10 +.4. The best viewpoints are just a quarter-mile off the blacktop and they'll give you a good overview of what's down below. Once down on the canyon floor, the swirls and cracks and chimneys and spires in the rocks become more evident—and also more three-dimensional. The surrounding red canyon walls contrast sharply to the patches of irrigated greenery in the Shivwits area (which is named after a local Indian tribe).

If you continue on past Shivwits for another mile and a half, you'll come to the southern boundary of the park and the end of Utah 300. Beyond that point the paved road becomes a "Scenic Backway" which you can follow to the town of Santa Clara and then back to Saint George. Or you can double-back up to the canyon rim and then north on Utah 18 for a mile to the volcanic area. A steep trail leads straight up the side of a good-sized cinder cone to the rim of the extinct volcano's crater.

🌲 **Utah 35** ♿

QUAIL CREEK
State Park

Location: Southwest corner of Utah northeast of St. George.

Access: From Utah State Highway 9 at a point 4 miles east of Interstate 15 Exit 16 and 5 miles west of Hurricane, turn north onto a paved access road and proceed 3 miles to the park.

Day Use Facilities: 2 medium-sized group pavilions (sun shelters) with drinking water and electricity; restrooms; (unreserved campsites may also be used by picnickers).

Overnight Facilities: 23 campsites; (2 group areas are also available for camping); sites are generally small to small+, with minimal to nominal separation; parking pads are gravel, medium-length straight-ins or long pull-throughs; a bit of additional leveling may be needed in some sites; adequate space for medium to large tents; ramadas (arched sun/wind shelters) in most sites; fire rings; b-y-o firewood; water at several faucets; restrooms; gravel driveways; complete supplies and services are available in St. George.

Activities & Attractions: Boating; boat launch; fishing for stocked trout, also bass and bluegill.

Natural Features: Located in a shallow basin near the west shore of Quail Creek Reservoir; park vegetation consists mostly of brush and tall grass and a few small planted trees; bordered by sage-covered low hills and ridges; elevation 3300´.

Season & Fees: Open all year; please see Appendix for reservation information and standard Utah state park entry and campground fees.

Mail & Phone: Quail Creek State Park, P.O. Box 1943, St. George, UT 84770; ☎(435) 879-2378.

Park Notes: Since this is high desert country, the park is more popular in spring and fall than in the very warm summer or surprisingly cool winter. However, if you're buzzing along the Interstate in midsummer and need a break, the park is only ten minutes or so from the freeway exit. There is sufficient shade from the small or large shelters as well as respectable desert lake vistas for a good lunch stop or coffee break. If you're camping, an airy tent or rv and a large tarp or awning would provide the most desirable shelter. There's often a good afternoon breeze here and it usually cools down after midnight. (There's only one other public campground in this corner of Utah which is handier from the Interstate—a BLM camp nestled up against red cliffs a few hundred yards west of the freeway. Nighttime warmth from the rocks is provided at no extra charge.)

▲ **Utah 36**

CORAL PINK SAND DUNES
State Park

Location: Southwest Utah east of St. George.

Access: From U.S. Highway 89 at mileposts 77 +.7 or 78 +.1 (13 miles northwest of Kanab, 6 miles southeast of Mt. Carmel Junction), turn southwest at either of the access points and proceed 0.2 mile on the frontage road to a 'Y' intersection; turn left or right (depending upon which approach you used) and proceed south on a paved local road for 11.5 miles; turn southeast (left) and continue for 0.1 mile to the park entrance station; the picnic area and campground are 0.3 mile beyond the entrance.

Day Use Facilities: Small picnic area with parking spaces.

Overnight Facilities: 22 campsites, including 3 double sites and a group site; sites are average to large, essentially level, with generally good separation; parking pads are paved, boulder-edged, mostly long pull-throughs; adequate sandy spots for large tents; concrete pads for many table areas; fire rings and barbecue grills; b-y-o firewood; water at several faucets; restrooms with showers; holding tank disposal station; paved driveway; limited supplies and services are available in Kanab.

Activities & Attractions: Sand dunes; hiking trails; orv (off road vehicle) exploration; self-guiding nature trail; small visitor center.

Natural Features: Located on a high plateau surrounded by sand dunes of an extraordinary coral-magenta color; a long, rocky, tree-dotted ridge borders the park on the east, a greener ridge is off to the south; picnic area and campground vegetation consists of medium to large junipers/cedars, piñon pines, yucca, sage, assorted desert plants and sparse grass; typically breezy; elevation 6000´.

Season & Fees: April to November; please see Appendix for reservation information and standard Utah state park entry and campground fees.

Mail & Phone: Coral Pink Sand Dunes State Park, P.O. Box 95, Kanab, UT 84741; ☎(435) 874-2408.

Park Notes: The park is geared to accommodating the needs of orv'rs, and you're asked to contact the park office prior to your trip, or at least upon arrival, in order to get the applicable regs for using a cycle, dune buggy, three-wheeler or whatever on the dunes and back roads. If you're afoot, there are millions of tons of warm sand to romp in (but watch out for low-flying duners). Photography is also a favorite diversion. The afternoon and evening sun, particularly, creates interesting and extremely photogenic shadowy effects on the already brightly hued dunes.

🌲 Utah 37 ♿

OTTER CREEK
State Park

Location: South-central Utah south of Richfield.

Access: From Utah State Highway 62 at milepost 11 +.8 (4 miles north of Antimony, 10 miles east of Kingston, 26 miles south of Koosharem), turn east onto Utah State Highway 22; proceed 0.5 mile, then turn north into the park.

Day Use Facilities: Small picnic area; drinking water; restrooms; large parking lot.

Overnight Facilities: 30 campsites; (31 overflow camping slots in parking lots on the east and west ends of the park are also available); sites are smallish, mostly level, with nil to minimal separation; parking pads are paved or gravel, small to medium-length straight-ins or parallel pull-throughs; 6 spots have large, framed, sandy tent pads; a number of sites have windbreaks; barbecue grills; b-y-o firewood; water at several faucets; restrooms with showers; holding tank disposal station; paved driveways; gas and groceries in Antimony.

Activities & Attractions: Boating; windsurfing; boat launch and docks; good to excellent fishing for rainbow trout; fish cleaning station; swimming beach.

Natural Features: Located on a narrow strip of land between the south shore of 2500-acre Otter Creek Reservoir and the highway; picnic and camp sites receive minimal to light shade from medium to large hardwoods and a few conifers on small plots of watered and mown lawns or sparse grass; most picnic and camp sites have views of the lake; the reservoir stretches for 5 miles up the broad valley between sage slopes and juniper-dotted mountains; maximum depth of the lake is about 40 feet, (depending upon precipitation inflow and summer drawdown outflow); typically breezy; elevation 6400´.

Season & Fees: Open all year; please see Appendix for reservation information and standard Utah state park entry and campground fees.

Mail & Phone: Otter Creek State Park, P.O. Box 43, Antimony, UT 84712; ☎ (435) 624-3268.

Park Notes: Otter Creek offers what probably is the most comprehensive set of water recreation opportunities in this area. (Piute State Park, located on Piute Reservoir, northwest of Otter Creek, off the east side of U.S. 89 north of the settlement of Junction, has good fishing but only primitive facilities.) Otter Creek produces a lot of good catches. Said one successful fisherman (who was cleaning a cooler full of good-sized trout at the time): "There are a few usual hot spots, but mostly the fish are wherever you find them". Sure. Locals as well as outsiders like it here, and the park commonly swells to capacity on summer weekends.

🏠 *Utah* 🏕
Southeast Canyons

🌲 Utah 38 ♿

KODACHROME BASIN
State Park

Location: South-central Utah southeast of Panguitch.

Access: From Utah State Highway 12 at milepost 25 +.8 on the east edge of the hamlet of Cannonville (26 miles southeast of the junction of Highway 12 and U.S Highway 89, 34 miles southwest of Escalante), turn southeast onto a paved local road and travel 7.2 miles to the end of the pavement (the thru road is gravel/dirt beyond this point); turn sharply north (left) onto the paved park access road and proceed 0.5 mile to the park entrance; continue ahead for 0.6 mile; turn northeast (right) onto a dirt road to Utah's Newest Arch and Chimney Rock, or continue ahead on the paved park road for 0.5 mile to the

Panorama Trailhead, 1 mile to the group area and 1.1 miles to the campground.

Day Use Facilities: Group picnic area.

Overnight Facilities: 24 campsites; sites are medium to large, with fair to good separation; parking pads are packed gravel, long pull-throughs or pull-offs; some additional leveling will be required in many sites; medium to large areas for tents; barbecue grills; b-y-o firewood; water at central faucets; restrooms with showers; packed gravel driveway; gas and groceries+ are available in Tropic, 5 miles west of Cannonville.

Activities & Attractions: Panorama Hiking Trail (3 miles over moderately rough terrain, allow 2 hours); Eagles View Overlook Trail (0.6 mile); nature trail (0.4-mile loop, guide pamphlet available); concession-operated horseback and buggy rides.

Natural Features: Located in a high desert environment amidst a collection of rock chimneys, spires, arches, monuments, pockets, arroyos and canyons; vegetation consists mostly of junipers/cedars, which provide minimal to light shade for picnic and camp sites, plus some pinyon pines, assorted brush and sparse grass; elevation 5800´.

Season & Fees: Open all year; campsite reservations accepted; please see Appendix for reservation information and standard Utah state park entry and campground fees.

Mail & Phone: Kodachrome Basin State Park, P.O. Box 238, Cannonville, UT 84718; ☎ (435) 679-8562.

Park Notes: The 'colorful' name for the park goes back to the September 1949 issue of National Geographic which called it "Kodachrome Flats" in an article about a National Geographic Society expedition into this area. The local Lions Club then adopted the name for a park which it had sponsored here for many years. However, it was rumored that Kodak wasn't exactly enchanted with the idea of using the name of its famous slide film for the park, so the obliging Lions changed the name to Chimney Rock Park. The Kodak folks responded, saying they really *liked* the use

of its name for the park, so the title was changed *back* to "Kodachrome". The local park later become a state reserve and eventually achieved full state park status.

Although Kodachrome Basin's scenic stature is overshadowed somewhat by nearby Bryce Canyon's sensational spectacles, it is a worthwhile side trip if you're in the vicinity. (Incidentally, a widely circulated park brochure suggests another side trip to view Grosvenor Arch as being "well worth the additional short drive" from Kodachrome Basin. Well, if you're determined to view the arch named for the late distinguished editor of *National Geographic*, it might be helpful to know that the "short drive" is on ten miles of gravel/dirt road that becomes really gunky when it gets wet.) A bonus to an overnight visit to Kodachrome Basin is its fine campground—one of the best public camps in these parts (and superior to Bryce's in most ways). The campground is in a large pocket nearly surrounded by some of the Basin's more interesting rock formations.

🔺 **Utah 39** ♿

ESCALANTE
State Park

Location: South-central Utah west of Escalante.

Access: From Utah State Highway 12 at milepost 58 +.3 (1.5 miles west of the town of Escalante, 45 miles east of Bryce Canyon National Park), turn north onto a gravel access road and proceed 0.7 mile to the park.

Day Use Facilities: Small picnic area; small parking lot; drinking water and restrooms in the adjacent campground.

Overnight Facilities: 22 campsites; (a group camp area is also available); sites are mostly average-sized, with minimal to nominal separation; parking pads are short to medium-length straight-ins, pull-throughs, or pull-offs; many pads may require additional leveling; some really good tent spots; a half-dozen sites have ramadas (sun shelters); barbecue grills and fire rings; firewood is sometimes provided, b-y-o to be sure; water at several faucets; restrooms with showers; holding tank disposal station; gravel driveway; limited supplies and services are available in Escalante.

Activities & Attractions: Boating; windsurfing; boat launch; fishing (said to be good) for trout and sunfish; adjacent petrified forest contains mineralized wood and fossilized dinosaur bones; Petrified Forest Trail; nature trail; footbridge over the creek; beautiful scenic views along Highway 12, especially approaching from the east; (you'll see some really vast vistas).

Natural Features: Located on sloping terrain above the east shore of 30-acre Wide Hollow Reservoir on the Escalante River, a few miles east of the Escalante Mountains; the 'infield' of the campground is a watered and mown lawn; some shade is provided by a few junipers/cedars and hardwoods; the park is set against a backdrop of red and beige cliffs; juniper-dotted bluffs surround the lake; elevation 5800´.

Season & Fees: Open all year; please see Appendix for reservation information and standard Utah state park entry and campground fees.

Mail & Phone: Escalante State Park, P.O. Box 350, Escalante, UT 84726; ☎(435) 826-4466.

Park Notes: This is a nice park for anywhere. But when you unexpectedly find it way out here about 90 miles from nowhere, it's not just nice, but a welcome oasis in this ruggedly beautiful, high desert country. The park previously was named "Escalante Petrified Forest State Park" in reference to one of its principal features. The present name, although more generic, is also less restrictive in relation to the park's multiple facets.

🌲 **Utah 40** ♿

ANASAZI
State Park

Location: South-central Utah in Boulder.

Access: From Utah State Highway 12 at milepost 87 + .8 (on the northern outskirts of the community of Boulder, 31 miles south of Torrey), turn east into the park.

Day Use Facilities: Small picnic area; drinking water and restrooms inside the visitor center; parking lot.

Overnight Facilities: None; nearest public campground is Calf Creek (Public Lands/BLM) 11 miles southwest of Boulder on Highway 12; also, several Dixie National Forest camps 19 to 25 miles north of Boulder on Highway 12.

Activities & Attractions: Self-guiding trail through excavated ruins of a prehistoric Anasazi Indian village with nearly 90 rooms; full-size, 6-room replica of an original dwelling; visitor center features informational exhibits and displays of artifacts relating to the culture of the Anasazi people, a diorama representing the original village, and audio-visual interpretive programs.

Natural Features: Located in hilly terrain near the south slopes of the forested Boulder Mountains; local vegetation consists of small pines, junipers/cedars and brush; elevation 6700´.

Season & Fees: Open all year; please see Appendix for standard Utah state park entry fees.

Mail & Phone: Anasazi State Park, P.O. Box 393, Boulder, UT 84716; ☎(435) 335-7308.

Park Notes: *Anasazi* is a Navajo word meaning "Ancient Ones" and it is used to describe the people of a fairly advanced civilization who lived throughout much of the Four Corners region of Arizona, Colorado, New Mexico and Utah for about the first 13 centuries A.D. The village discovered here is thought to have been one of the largest Anasazi settlements west of the Colorado River. Some 200 of the Ancient Ones lived and worked here from roughly 1050 to 1200 A.D. Most of the tools, pottery, and other items of everyday living which are on display in the visitor center were unearthed in this village. The Indians here are said to have been fairly well off by comparison to those in other communities.

It remains a mystery why the entire Anasazi culture disappeared sometime during the thirteenth century. Were the Anasazi victims of climatic change, famine or disease; were they vanquished by enemies and assimilated into their conquerors' culture; did they exhaust their regional resources and then emigrate *en masse* to a faraway land? (Or, as has been seriously suggested, were many of them whisked away to another world by benevolent interplanetary travelers?) As you visit this park and the dozen or more others in the Southwest which present as much of the saga of the Anasazi as is known, you might begin to form your own theory.

▲ Utah 41 &

HUNTINGTON
State Park

Location: Central Utah south of Price.

Access: From Utah State Highway 10 at milepost 49 +.4 (2 miles north of Huntington, 19 miles south of Price), turn west onto State Highway 155 and proceed 0.2 mile; turn south into the park entrance.

Day Use Facilities: Medium-sized picnic area; large pavilion (sun shelter), available for group use by reservation; drinking water; restrooms; parking lot.

Overnight Facilities: 22 campsites; sites are medium-sized, essentially level, with minimal separation; parking pads are medium to long, paved straight-ins or pull-offs; excellent, large, grassy tent spots; fireplaces; b-y-o firewood; water at several faucets; restrooms with showers; holding tank disposal station; paved driveways; limited to adequate supplies and services are available in Huntington.

Activities & Attractions: Large, grassy beach; swimming area; fishing (said to be very good) for largemouth bass, also bluegill; boating; boat launch; walking/jogging on service roads around the reservoir; Cleveland-Lloyd Dinosaur Quarry (operated by the BLM), 20 miles east.

Natural Features: Located on the east shore of 250-acre Huntington Lake (Reservoir); park vegetation consists of some medium to tall hardwoods on spacious, watered and mown lawns; surrounded by a desert plain and reclaimed agricultural land; mountains and mesas of the Wasatch Plateau lie to the near west; mountains of the San Rafael Swell are visible in the distant east; elevation 5800´.

Season & Fees: Open all year; please see Appendix for reservation information and standard Utah state park entry and campground fees.

Mail & Phone: Huntington State Park, P.O. Box 1343, Huntington, UT 84528; ☎ (435) 687-2491.

Park Notes: To say that the grounds look 'manicured' in the true sense of the word wouldn't be overstating things by much. All picnic sites and about half of the campsites have lake views. Nice park. A couple of good side trips which might make staying here even more worthwhile are also worth mentioning. Taking a liesurely drive up State Highway 31 northwest out of the town of Huntington will get you into the very high, green country of the Wasatch Plateau. A somewhat more challenging excursion is the one out to the dino site east of Cleveland. There's a small visitor center there with exhibits, a picnic area, and the big boneyard where so far they've dug up enough parts for 30 complete critters, plus about 10,000 more bones from about 100 different prehistoric animals. About three-fourths of the 20-mile trip is on gravel/dirt roads, so it isn't just a quick jaunt out and back. It would be prudent to call the BLM district office in Moab for current info on days and hours of operation and to get detailed directions to the site.

▲ Utah 42 &

MILLSITE
State Park

Location: Central Utah south of Price.

Access: From Utah State Highway 10 at milepost 26 +.7 in the community of Ferron (27 miles north of Interstate 70 Exit 89, 41 miles south of Price), turn west (at the national forest ranger station) onto Ferron Canyon Road (paved); travel west for 4.2 miles; turn north onto the park access road, and proceed 0.2 mile to the park.

Day Use Facilities: Small picnic area; 2 medium-sized pavilions (sun shelters); 2 small parking areas; other facilities shared with campground.

Overnight Facilities: 20 campsites; sites are small to medium-sized, level, with minimal separation; parking pads are medium to long straight-ins or pull-throughs; adequate space for medium to large tents in many units; barbecue grills; b-y-o firewood; water at several faucets; restrooms with showers; holding tank disposal station; limited supplies and services are available in Ferron.

Activities & Attractions: Fishing for stocked rainbow and cutthroat trout; boating; boat launch and dock; sandy beach; nature trail; 9-hole municipal golf course, adjacent to the park.

Natural Features: Located on the slightly sloping south shore of 450-acre Millsite Reservoir, an impoundment on Ferron Creek; park vegetation consists primarily of young hardwoods and sections of watered lawns; surroundings are starkly desertish; a barren, 2000´ escarpment along the east edge of the Wasatch Plateau borders one side of the reservoir; elevation 6100´.

Season & Fees: Open all year; please see Appendix for reservation information and standard Utah state park entry and campground fees.

Mail & Phone: c/o Huntington State Park, P.O. Box 1343, Huntington, UT 84528; ☎ (435) 687-2491.

Park Notes: Although quite a few trees have been planted, they still don't provide an abundance of shade, so it might be a good idea to pack an extra tarp or a beach umbrella to keep off the excess rays in this sunny climate. Many of the poplars here are transplants from another state park which had an excess of foliage; the sand on the beach was hauled in from Great Salt Lake. The reservoir was named for a logging mill which formerly stood near here.

Millsite is a satellite unit of nearby Huntington State Park. Although both parks are comparably landscaped, at roughly similar elevations, and only 20 miles apart, they each have enough of their own distinctive characteristics which might make you prefer one over the other. Millsite is several easy miles off the highway; Huntington offers 20-second access just off the main drag. Millsite Reservoir has a greater volume than Huntington and consequently the water temperature remains colder through the region's hot summers; trout like Millsite, but bass, swimmers and waterskiers prefer warmer Huntington. Huntington is on a desert plain and has fine distant views in all directions; Millsite is closely bordered by barren slopes and very imposing high cliffs. Heads or tails?

▲ Utah 43 ♿

GREEN RIVER
State Park

Location: East-central Utah in Green River.

Access: From Interstate 70 (eastbound) Exit 158, travel east on Business Route I-70/Main Street for 1.6 miles into midtown Green River; at the intersection of Main Street and Green River Boulevard, turn south (right) onto Green River Boulevard and proceed 0.5 mile, then turn east (left) for 0.1 mile to the park; **Alternate Access:** From I-70 (westbound), take Exit 162, then go west on Business I-70/Main Street for 2.6 miles to Green River Boulevard and continue as above.

Day Use Facilities: Small picnic area; group pavilion; drinking water; restrooms; medium-sized parking lot.

Overnight Facilities: 40 campsites in 2 loops; sites are medium+ in size, level, with minimal to nominal separation; parking pads are paved, medium to long straight-ins; plenty of space for a large tent in most sites; assorted fire appliances; b-y-o firewood; water at faucets throughout; restrooms with showers; holding tank disposal station; paved driveways; adequate supplies and services are available in Green River.

Activities & Attractions: River floating; boat launch; fishing; 9-hole golf course;

small amphitheater; rockhounding (said to be very good) for agate, geodes, jasper and petrified wood on public lands in the vicinity; annual 200-mile Friendship Cruise from Green River to Moab begins at the state park.

Natural Features: Located on a large flat along the west bank of the Green River; all sites have a fair to good amount of shade/shelter provided by mature hardwoods on watered, mown lawns; arid, high, rocky terrain surrounds the park; park area is 63 acres; elevation 4100´.

Season & Fees: Open all year; greens fees $7.00; please see Appendix for reservation information and standard Utah state park entry and campground fees.

Mail & Phone: Green River State Park, P.O. Box 93, Green River, UT 84525; ☎(435) 564-3633.

Park Notes: Although Indians had traveled through this region for centuries and the Spanish had begun exploring the Southwest in 1540, the history of the Green River was not initiated until 1776. In that year, those intrepid explorers of the Southwest, Friars Dominguez and Escalante, first led a small group through this region and discovered the Green River, which they named the *Rio San Buenaventura*, at the site of the present-day city of Green River.

Nearly a century later, Major John Wesley Powell, an intelligent, gutsy, one-armed Civil War veteran, led an expedition with nine men and four rowboats through here during one of the West's greatest epics of exploration. Powell and his band left a launch site at Green River, Wyoming in late May 1869, floated the Green through Flaming Gorge, the Canyon of Ledore (which they called "Hell's Half Mile"), Desolation Canyon, and emerged from Gray Canyon, near here, on July 13. They camped under cottonwoods along the banks of the Green, possibly where you might be picnicking or camping in the state park.

Powell and his crew continued on down the Green and Colorado Rivers through a succession of canyons which Powell named Labyrinth, Cataract, Glen, Marble, and Grand until, on August 29/30, they exited Grand Canyon at what is now Lake Mead.

As you approach the Green River area in four-lane, mile-a-minute, air-conditioned leisure and comfort, imagine what it must have been like .....

▲ Utah 44 &

GOBLIN VALLEY
State Park

Location: South-central Utah southwest of Green River.

Access: From Utah State Highway 24 at Temple Mountain Junction (21 miles northeast of Hanksville, 24 miles southwest of Interstate 40 Exit 147 west of Green River), turn west onto a paved local road and travel west/northwest for 7 miles; turn southwest (left) onto a gravel/dirt road and proceed another 7 miles to the park. (The last 7-mile stretch of road is generally quite passable, except for periods during, or within a few days after, a rain or snow; it might be a good idea to call Green River State Park for current info about road and park conditions.)

Day Use Facilities: Small picnic area; other facilities shared with campground.

Overnight Facilities: 21 campsites; sites are small, basically level and closely spaced; parking spaces are gravel, short+ straight-ins; small tent areas; barbecue grills; b-y-o firewood; water at central faucets; restrooms with showers; holding tank disposal station; gravel driveways; gas and groceries in Hanksville; adequate supplies and services are available in Green River.

Activities & Attractions: Views and viewpoints of the valley; ramada at observation point; open hiking among the rock forms; literally hundreds of miles of 4wd roads and trails lead to even more remote places in the region.

Natural Features: Located in a deep, high-desert valley which contains dozens of rock shapes whittled by wind and water to form curiously carved creatures of stone; park vegetation consists mainly of sparse grass and small brush and other desert plants; park area is 3654 acres; elevation 5200´.

Season & Fees: Open all year; please see Appendix for reservation information and standard Utah state park entry and campground fees.

Mail & Phone: c/o Green River State Park, P.O. Box 93, Green River, UT 84525; ☎(435) 564-3633.

Park Notes: Goblin Valley was originally called "Mushroom Valley" by local explorers because so many of the smaller, upright, eroded rock forms resembled the fancy fungus, (although this sunstruck, parched land is anything *but* mushroom country.) For that matter, some of the formations look like chess pieces. (It all depends upon the time of day, the breadth and depth of your own imagination, and maybe even what beverage you had with your dinner.)

Electricity to operate this remote park's water pumps and lights is generated entirely by a 1.4 kilowatt solar array channeling the sun's energy to a large bank of rechargeable batteries. The system stores enough juice for about three days normal use. (That's an adequate backup supply because the sun shines *a lot* around here.) Hot water for the restrooms is solar-heated, but by a different device. The high-tech, no-noise approach sure beats the 15kw clackety diesel power pumper which was replaced by the solar methods. It's particularly welcome in this tranquil, far-out, near-wilderness location. Ironically, the money that paid for the solar energy system came from the settlement of a federal court case involving price gouging by an oil company.

▲ Utah 45

DEAD HORSE POINT
State Park

Location: Southeast Utah southwest of Moab.

Access: From U.S. Highway 191 at milepost 136 +.8 (12 miles northwest of Moab, 21 miles south of Interstate 70 Exit 180 at Crescent Junction), turn west onto Utah State Highway 313 (paved); travel west and south on this sometimes steep and winding road for 22 miles to the park entrance; proceed for another 0.3 mile to the campground; or continue for another mile past the campground to the day use area at Dead Horse Point.

Day Use Facilities: Medium-sized picnic area; large ramada (sun shelter); medium-sized parking lot.

Overnight Facilities: 20 campsites; (a large group camp area is also available, by reservation); sites are medium to large, with fairly good separation; parking pads are gravel, mostly medium to long straight-ins, plus several long pull-throughs; a few pads may require a little additional leveling; medium to large, acceptably level tent spaces; sites have ramadas (sun/partial wind shelters) with lighted table areas on concrete pads; barbecue grills; b-y-o firewood; water at several faucets; restrooms; holding tank disposal station; paved driveway; adequate supplies and services are available in Moab.

Activities & Attractions: Some of the finest canyon views in the Desert Southwest; visitor center with interpretive exhibits; hiking trails; nature trail (a nice guide booklet is available); the expansive Island in the Sky region of Canyonlands National Park lies a few miles west of the state park.

Natural Features: Located on the edge of a plateau overlooking Meander Canyon and the Colorado River, nearly 2000´ below; local vegetation consists primarily of clump grass, small bushes and brush, and the ever-present juniper/cedar; elevation 5700´.

Season & Fees: Open all year, with limited services October to April; please see Appendix for reservation information and standard Utah state park entry and campground fees.

Mail & Phone: Dead Horse Point State Park, P.O. Box 609, Moab, UT 84532; ☎(435) 259-6511.

Park Notes: The name of this distant place stems from a tragic incident many years ago when a band of wild horses was corralled at the point, and left by their captors without food or water. This isn't just a side trip—it's an adventure. Part of the first half-dozen miles on the state highway consists of switchbacks and steep grades. But don't let that discourage you. The road levels-out shortly, and traverses the top of the plateau to the Point. What you'll see along the way, and at your destination, really should be seen and felt and *experienced*—and not merely read about.

▲ Utah 46 ♿

EDGE OF THE CEDARS
State Park

Location: Southwest Utah in Blanding.

Access: From U.S. Highway 191 just north of midtown Blanding (21 miles south of Monticello), turn west onto 400 North and proceed 0.4 mile; the park is at 660 West 400 North.

Day Use Facilities: Small picnic area; drinking water and restrooms inside the museum; small parking area.

Overnight Facilities: None; nearest public campground is Devils Canyon (Manti-La Sal National Forest), 10 miles north of Blanding on U.S. 191.

Activities & Attractions: Museum with Indian artifacts and informational exhibits about the cultures which have affected the development of southeast Utah: the prehistoric Anasazi, the Navajo and the Ute, and European-Americans; auditorium; modern Indian crafts shop and demonstration area; self-guided walks of the partially excavated ruins of a small Anasazi village west of the museum.

Natural Features: Located in a stone and mortar building and on a ridge top just west of the museum above Westwater Canyon; bordered by juniper/cedar-dotted plains and hills; elevation 6200´.

Season & Fees: Open all year; please see Appendix for standard Utah state park entry fees.

Mail & Phone: Edge of the Cedars State Park, P.O. Box 788, Blanding, UT 84511; ☎ (435) 678-2238.

Park Notes: The prehistoric hamlet associated with the museum was inhabited during a 500-year period ending in the early thirteenth century by the Anasazi, a people who lived in this region for more than a millennium and then vanished. The small village contains six clusters of structures, each with rectangular rooms and circular ceremonial *kivas*. The museum is especially noted for having one of the largest Anasazi pottery collections in the Southwest. It also has the only known metal artifact used by the Utah Anasazi, which was essentially a stone age culture.

▲ Utah 47

GOOSENECKS
State Park

Location: Southeast corner of Utah northwest of Mexican Hat.

Access: From Utah State Highway 261 near milepost 1 (1 mile west of the junction of Highway 261 & U.S. Highway 163 north of Mexican Hat, 31 miles south of the junction of State Highways 261 & 276 near Natural Bridges National Monument), turn west onto State Highway 316 and travel 3.8 miles west/southwest to the park.

Day Use Facilities: Small picnic/camp area with shared facilities.

Overnight Facilities: Approximately 3 camp/picnic sites; (or adequate room for perhaps 8-10 campers in an 'open' camping arrangement); ample space for large vehicles; not really suitable for tents unless they're free-standing and heavily weighted; ramada (sun shelter); no drinking water; vault facilities; gas and camper supplies in Mexican Hat.

Activities & Attractions: Viewpoint.

Natural Features: Located on the rim of a canyon overlooking the San Juan River; vegetation consists primarily of desert brush and sparse grass; red bluffs and cliffs and a desert plain border the area; typically windy; elevation 4500´.

Season & Fees: Open all year; no fee (subject to change).

Mail & Phone: c/o Edge of the Cedars State Park, P.O. Box 788, Blanding, UT 84511; ☎ (435) 678-2238.

Park Notes: As you stand on the brink of the chasm, a thousand feet below your boots the San Juan River tightly switchbacks several times on its course to meet the Colorado River many miles downstream. In order to travel a single horizontal mile westerly as the crow or the hawk flies, the silty stream twists and turns and doubles back around for more than five river miles.

As long as you're in the neighborhood, another series of local switchbacks may be of interest to you. On Highway 261, about 5 miles northwest of the Goosenecks turnoff, there's an overlook point which provides a stupendous view of the great valley that borders the San Juan Canyon. The highway is very steep and very twisty and very narrow in this section, but the visual reward from traveling the route probably would be worth a few minutes of white-knuckle driving (assuming you're in a type of transport that's up to the task). One of the places far below the overlook point is the small community of Mexican Hat—named for the sombrero-shaped rock that does a roadside balancing act just north of town.

Notes & Sketches

⛺ SPECIAL SECTION ⛺

Creative Traveling

In its most elementary form, traveling requires very little in the way of extensive planning or highly specialized and sophisticated equipment. A stout knife, some matches, a few blankets, a free road map, a water jug, and a sack of p.b.& j. sandwiches, all tossed onto the seat of an old beater pickup, will get you started on the way to a lifetime of outdoor adventures.

Idyllic and nostalgic as that scenario may seem, most of the individuals reading this *Double Eagle*™ Guide (as well as those *writing* it) probably desire (and deserve) at least a few granules of comfort sprinkled over their car or mini van, and around their tent or rv.

There are enough books already on the market or in libraries which will provide you with plenty of advice on *how* to travel.In this series we've concentrated your hard-earned *dinero* into finding out *where* to travel. However, there are still a few items that aren't widely known, or which bear repeating, so we've included them in the following paragraphs.

Resourcefulness. When putting together your equipment, it's both challenging and a lot of fun to make the ordinary stuff you have around the house, especially in the kitchen, do double duty. Offer an 'early retirement' to serviceable utensils, pans, plastic cups, etc. to a 'gear box'.

Resource-fullness. Empty plastic peanut butter jars, pancake syrup and milk jugs, ketchup bottles, also aluminum pie plates and styrofoam trays, can be washed, re-labeled and used again. (The syrup jugs, with their handles and pop-up spouts, make terrific 'canteens' for kids.) The lightweight, break-resistant plastic stuff is more practical on a camping trip than glass containers, anyway. *El Cheapo* plastic shopping bags, which have become *de rigueur* in supermarkets, can be saved and re-used to hold travel litter and picnic or camping trash. When they're full, tie them tightly closed using the 'handles'.

Redundancy. Whether you're traveling in a car, pickup, van, boat, motorhome or trailer, it pays to think and plan like a backpacker. Can you make-do with fewer changes of clothes for a short weekend trip? How about getting-by with half as much diet cola, and drink more cool, park spring water instead? Do you really *need* that third curling iron? Real backpackers (like the guy who trimmed the margins off his maps) are relentless in their quest for the light load.

Water. No matter where you travel, *always* carry a couple of gallons of drinking water. Backwoods water sources may be out of order (e.g., someone broke the handle off the hydrant or the well went dry). Because of the possibility of encountering the widespread 'beaver fever' (*Giardia lamblia*) parasite and other diseases in lakes and streams, if treated or tested H_2O isn't available, boil the surface water for a full five minutes.

Juice. If you're a tent or small vehicle camper who normally doesn't need electrical hookups, carry a hotplate, coffee pot, or hair dryer when traveling in regions where hookup campsites are available. The trend in public campground management is toward charging the full rate for a hookup site whether or not you have an rv, even though there are no standard sites available for you to occupy. In many popular state parks, hookup sites far outnumber standard sites. At least you'll have some use for the juice.

Fire. A really handy, clean option to using wood or charcoal is to carry a couple of synthetic 'fire logs'. The sawdust-and-paraffin logs are made from byproducts of the lumber and petroleum industries and burn about three hours in the outdoors. The fire logs can also be used to start and maintain a regular picnic or camp fire if the locally gathered firewood is wet.

Styrofoam. This flimsy synthetic may not be environmentally acceptable, but it's a fact of modern life. After you stop for a fuel-up and a rest break along the highway, save the foam cups which contained your coffee, cocoa or soft drinks; then rinse them out at the next stop or when you arrive at your picnic or camp site. The cups can be used again for drinks, collecting specimens for nature study, or to hold nightcrawlers gathered from under a log for fishing bait.

Styrofoam or paper cups weighted with a few stones occasionally can be seen holding a small collection of wildflowers and left on the picnic table as a centerpiece for the next visitors.

Rattlers. Anywhere you go in the West, expect to find rattlesnakes or other poisonous reptiles, so place your hands and feet and other vital parts accordingly. (While preparing the *Double Eagle*™ series, one of the publishers inadvertently poked her zoom lens to within a yard of a coiled rattler's snout. The photographer's anxieties were vocally, albeit shakily, expressed; the level of stress which the incident induced on the snake is unknown.)

Mosquitoes. The winged demons aren't usually mentioned in the text because you just have to *expect* them almost anywhere except perhaps in the driest desert areas. Soggy times, like late spring and early summer, are the worst times. If you're one of us who's always the first to be strafed by the local mosquito squadron, keep plenty of anti-aircraft ammo on hand. The most versatile skin stuff is the spray-on variety. Spray it all over your clothes to keep the varmints from poking their proboscis through the seat of your jeans. A room spray comes in handy for blasting any bugs which might have infiltrated your car, tent or rv. Fortunately, in most areas the peak of the mosquito season lasts only a couple of weeks, and you can enjoy yourself the rest of the time. Autumn traveling is great!

Plants. Poison ivy, oak and sumac can be found in many wooded regions throughout the West. Avoid off-trail brush-busting or side-swiping trailside vegetation with bare skin. Oleander, those beautifully flowering bushes planted in parks all over the Western Sunbelt are toxic, so keep your pets and your kids from nibbling on them. Likewise, in the desert regions, steer plenty clear of cholla cactus. The Indians call it the "jumping cactus" with good reason.

Creepy-crawlers. In arid Desert Southwest regions, watch for scorpions and other ground-based critters. In the Southwest Plains, tarantulas make their appearances in spring and fall, but the fuzzy arachnids will leave you alone if you reciprocate.

Horsepower. Your vehicle will lose about four percent of its power for each 1000´ gain in altitude above sea level. Keep that in mind in relation to the "pack like a backpacker" item mentioned previously. You might also keep it in mind when you embark on a foot trip. The factory-original human machine loses about the same amount of efficiency at higher elevations.

Air. To estimate the temperature at a park in the mountains while you're still down in the valley or on the plains, subtract about three degrees Fahrenheit for each 1000´ difference in elevation between the valley and the park. Use the same method to estimate nighttime lows in the mountains by using weather forecasts for valley cities.

Reptile repellent. Here's a sensitive subject. With the rise in crimes perpetrated against travelers in the nation's parks and forests and on its highways and byways, it's become increasingly common for legitimate travelers to pack a 'heater'—the type that's measured by caliber or gauge, not in volts and amps. To quote a respected Wyoming peace officer: "Half the pickups and campers in Wyoming and Montana have a .45 automatic under the seat or a 12-gauge pump beneath the bunk". If personal safety is a concern to you, check the laws, get competent instruction, practice a lot, and join the NRA.

Vaporhavens. Be skeptical when you scan highway and forest maps and see hundreds of little symbols which indicate the locations of alleged parks and campsites; or when you glance through listings published by government agencies or promotional interests. A high percentage of those 'recreation areas' are as vaporous as the mist rising from a warm lake into chilled autumn air. Many, many of the listed spots are actually simple picnic areas, fishing access sites, and even highway rest stops; dozens of camps are ill-maintained remnants of their former greatness, located at the end of rocky jeep trails; many others no longer exist; still others *never* existed, but are merely a mapmaker's or recreational planner's notion of where a recreation area *might* or *should* be. Make certain that a park exists and what it offers before you embark on 20 miles of washboard gravel travel in the never-ending quest for your own personal Eden.

We hope the foregoing items, and information throughout this series, help you conserve your own valuable time, money, fuel and other irreplaceable resources. ***Good Traveling!***

🏠 Appendix ⛺

Desert Southwest Standard State Park Fees

◾ Arizona

Daily park entry fee for most parks	$5.00-$9.00
Primitive/undeveloped campsite	$9.00
Standard/developed campsite	$10.00-$16.00
Hookup campsite	$19.00-$25.00
Cabana site	$19.00-$25.00
Cabins and yurts	$35.00-$75.00

◾ New Mexico

Daily park entry fee for most parks	$3.00-$5.00
Primitive campsite	$8.00
Standard/developed campsite	$10.00
Electrical hookup site	$14.00
Full hookup/sewer site	$18.00

◾ Utah

Daily park entry fee for most parks	$3.00-$5.00
Primitive campsite	$8.00
Standard/developed campsite (Flush restrooms)	$11.00
Standard/developed campsite (Flush restrooms & showers)	$14.00
Electrical hookup campsite	$17.00
Full hookup campsite	$20.00

(Campsite fee includes park entry fee.)

(A nominal discount is given on Utah fees for camping Sunday through Thursday nights.)

Fees for the use of group facilities and for special activities like golf courses and boat moorage vary considerably. As an example, expect to pay a minimum of $15.00 for a small group picnic to $125.00 for a large gathering, plus a substantial (but refundable) cleaning deposit. All states offer discount permits for handicapped individuals and seniors.

📄 *Desert Southwest State Park Reservations*

Reservations may be made for certain individual and group campsites in state parks in Arizona, New Mexico and Utah. As a general rule-of-thumb, reservations for midsummer weekends should be initiated at least several weeks in advance. Reservation fees are charged.

Reservations for individual and group campsites in *Utah* state parks may be obtained by calling the Utah State Parks office:

☎ **(800)-322-3770** (toll-free from outside Salt Lake City)
☎ **322-3770** (from within Salt Lake City)

For online *Utah* reservations, see the website: 🖳 **http://www.reserveamerica.com**

A service fee of $6.00 for an individual site and $12.00 for a group site is charged for each reservation. Reservations for individual campsites may be made from 3 days, to a maximum of 120 days, in advance; reservations for group sites may be made up to a year in advance.

Reservations are available for certain individual campsites in *Elephant Butte State Park* in *New Mexico*. Contact the park office at ☎(505) 744-5421. A reservation fee of $7.00 is charged.

Reservations for the following areas must be obtained directly from the selected state park. Additional specific information and procedures will be provided upon initial contact.

> • Group picnic sites, camp sites and other group facilities in Arizona
> • Group picnic and camp sites in New Mexico
> • Group picnic sites and other group facilities (except group campsites) in Utah

Reservable campsites are usually assigned, but you can request an rv or a tent site; rv sites are generally a little larger and most will accommodate tents. When making a reservation, be prepared to tell the reservation agent about the major camping equipment you plan to use, (size and number of tents, type and length of rv, additional vehicles, boat trailers, etc.). Be generous in your estimate. In most cases, a park's *best sites* are also those which are *reservable*. Most of the parks which have reservable sites still can accommodate a limited number of drop-ins on a first-come, first-served basis.

For additional information about picnic or camp site reservations, availability, current conditions, or regulations about the use of state parks, we suggest that you contact your selected park directly, using the *Mail & Phone* information in the text.

These offices might also be helpful:

Arizona

Arizona State Parks
1300 West Washington
Phoenix, AZ 85007
☎(602) 542-4174   🖳 http://www.pr.state.az.us

New Mexico

New Mexico State Parks and Recreation Division
408 Galisteo
Santa Fe, NM 87504
☎(505) 827-7465   🖳 http://www.emnrd.state.nm.us/prd/
☎(800)-451-2541 (from within New Mexico, toll-free)

Utah

Utah Division of Parks and Recreation
1636 West Temple, Suite 116
Salt Lake City, UT 84116
☎(801) 538-7220   🖳 http://www.stateparks.utah.gov/

Please remember that all fees and reservation information are subject to change without notice.

Arizona

♦ St. George, UT   ♦ Kanab, UT

♦ Page   ♦ Kayenta

Jacob Lake

15

Lake Mead

Boulder City
NV

North Rim   ♦ Tuba City   Chinle

89

♦ Cameron

Grand Canyon VIllage

Colorado River

San Francisco Mtns

8 Riordan   Flagstaff

Bullhead
City   Kingman

14 Homolovi Ruins

40

9 Slide Rock

11 Dead Horse Ranch   Sedona

12 Jerome   Winslow

40

10 Red Rock   Holbrook

Needles
CA

40

13 Fort Verde

16 Lyman Lake

Prescott

15 Fool Hollow Lake   Springerville

Lake Havasu City
1-2 Lake Havasu

89   **17**

Payson   Show Low

5 Alamo Lake

60   Alpine

3-4 Buckskin Mountain   Wickenburg

60

17 Lost Dutchman

Phoenix   Globe

Parker

Quartzite   **10**

18 Boyce Thompson

Blythe, CA   **10**   Casa Grande

19 McFarland   **70**   Morenci

Colorado River

Gila Bend

8   Safford

20 Picacho Peak   *22 Roper Lake*

21 Catalina

Yuma   Tucson   **10**

6 Yuma Territorial Prison   ♦ Ajo   Willcox

7 Yuma Quartermaster Depot

19   *26 Kartchner Caverns*

25 Tombstone Courthouse

23 Tubac Presidio   *Chiricahua Mtns.*

24 Patagonia Lake

Nogales

New Mexico

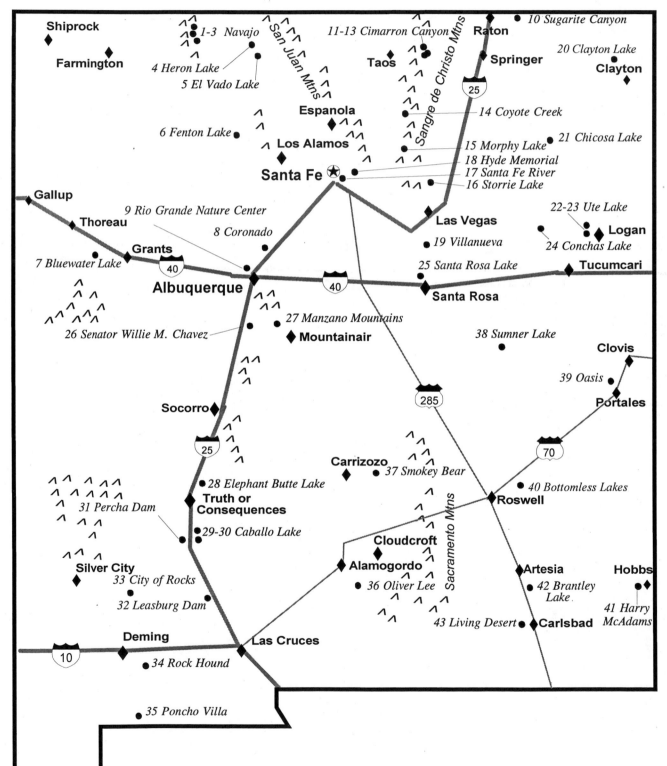

N

Shiprock
Farmington

1-3 Navajo
4 Heron Lake
5 El Vado Lake

San Juan Mtns

6 Fenton Lake

Espanola
Los Alamos
Santa Fe

11-13 Cimarron Canyon Raton
10 Sugarite Canyon
Taos Springer
20 Clayton Lake
Clayton

Sangre de Christo Mtns

14 Coyote Creek
15 Morphy Lake *21 Chicosa Lake*
18 Hyde Memorial
17 Santa Fe River
16 Storrie Lake

Gallup
9 Rio Grande Nature Center
Thoreau
8 Coronado
Grants
7 Bluewater Lake

Albuquerque

Las Vegas
19 Villanueva
22-23 Ute Lake
Logan
24 Conchas Lake
25 Santa Rosa Lake Tucumcari
Santa Rosa

26 Senator Willie M. Chavez
27 Manzano Mountains
Mountainair

38 Sumner Lake
Clovis
39 Oasis
Portales

Socorro

Carrizozo
37 Smokey Bear

40 Bottomless Lakes
Roswell

28 Elephant Butte Lake
Truth or
Consequences
31 Percha Dam
29-30 Caballo Lake

Cloudcroft
Sacramento Mtns

Silver City
33 City of Rocks
32 Leasburg Dam

Alamogordo
36 Oliver Lee

Artesia
42 Brantley Lake
Hobbs

43 Living Desert Carlsbad
41 Harry McAdams

Deming
34 Rock Hound
Las Cruces

35 Poncho Villa

Utah

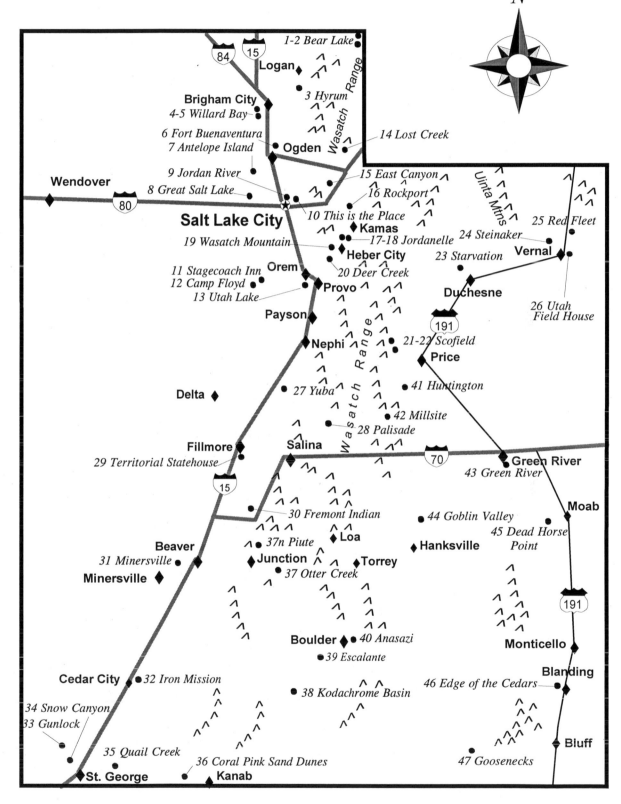

N

1-2 Bear Lake

Logan

Brigham City
4-5 Willard Bay

6 Fort Buenaventura
7 Antelope Island

3 Hyrum

Wasatch Range

14 Lost Creek

Ogden

Wendover

9 Jordan River
8 Great Salt Lake

15 East Canyon

16 Rockport

Uinta Mtns

25 Red Fleet

Salt Lake City

10 This is the Place

24 Steinaker

Vernal

19 Wasatch Mountain

Kamas

17-18 Jordanelle

23 Starvation

Heber City

11 Stagecoach Inn
12 Camp Floyd
13 Utah Lake

Orem

20 Deer Creek

Duchesne

Provo

191

26 Utah
Field House

Payson

Nephi

21-22 Scofield

Price

Delta

27 Yuba

41 Huntington

Wasatch Range

42 Millsite

28 Palisade

Fillmore

Salina

70

Green River

29 Territorial Statehouse

43 Green River

15

Moab

30 Fremont Indian

44 Goblin Valley

45 Dead Horse
Point

Beaver

37n Piute

Loa

Hanksville

31 Minersville

Junction

Torrey

Minersville

37 Otter Creek

191

Boulder

40 Anasazi

39 Escalante

Monticello

Cedar City

32 Iron Mission

Blanding

46 Edge of the Cedars

34 Snow Canyon
33 Gunlock

38 Kodachrome Basin

35 Quail Creek

36 Coral Pink Sand Dunes

Bluff

47 Goosenecks

St. George

Kanab

Notes & Sketches

INDEX

Important Note:

* A thumbnail description of a state park marked with an asterisk is found in the *Park Notes* section of the principal numbered state park.

Utah

Notes & Sketches

The Double Eagle Guide to

⚊ Camping *in* Western Parks *and* Forests 🚐

__*Volume 1* **Pacific Northwest**   ISBN 1-932417-31-1
         Washington ＊ Oregon   Hardcover $21.95＊

__*Volume 2* **Far West**   ISBN 1-932417-32-X
         Northern California ＊ Southern California＊Lake Tahoe Hardcover $21.95＊

__*Volume 3* **Desert Southwest**   ISBN 1-932417-33-8
         Nevada ＊ Utah ＊ Arizona   Hardcover $21.95＊

__*Volume 4* **Northern Rocky Mountains**   ISBN 1-932417-34-6
         Montana ＊ Idaho ＊ Wyoming   Hardcover $21.95＊

__*Volume 5* **Southern Rocky Mountains**   ISBN 1-932417-35-4
         Colorado ＊ New Mexico   Hardcover $21.95＊

__*Volume 6* **Northern Great Plains**   ISBN 1-932417-36-2
         North Dakota ＊ South Dakota ＊ Nebraska ＊ Kansas Hardcover $21.95＊

__*Volume 7* **Southern Great Plains**   ISBN 1-932417-37-0
         Texas ＊ Oklahoma   Hardcover $21.95＊

＊ **Save $3.00** Softcover, spiral-bound editions are also available. Recommended for light-duty, personal use only. Subtract $3.00 from the standard hardcover price and ✓here: ❑

Please add $4.00 for shipping the first volume, and $2.00 for each additional volume.

Please include your check/money order in the amount of _____

Name_____

Address_____

City_____ State_____ Zip_____

Please mail your completed order to:

Discovery Publishing   P.O. Box 50545   Billings, MT 59105   (Phone 1-406-861-6564)

Thank You Very Much For Your Order!

Prices, shipping charges, and specifications are subject to change.

(A photocopy or other reproduction may be substituted for this original form.)

The Double Eagle Guide to
▲ WESTERN STATE PARKS 🏚

__Volume 1   Pacific Northwest   ISBN 978-1-932417-15-9
            Washington*Oregon*Idaho   Hardcover 8½x11 $21.95^

__Volume 2   Rocky Mountains   ISBN 978-1-932417-16-6
            Colorado*Montana*Wyoming   Hardcover 8½x11 $21.95^

__Volume 3   Far West   ISBN 978-1-932417-16-6
            California*Nevada   Hardcover 8½x11 $21.95^

__Volume 4   Desert Southwest   ISBN 978-1-932417-18-0
            Arizona*New Mexico*Utah   Hardcover 8½x11 $21.95^

__Volume 5   Northern Great Plains   ISBN 978-1-932417-19-7
            The Dakotas*Nebraska*Kansas   Hardcover 8½x11 $21.95^

__Volume 6   Southern Great Plains   ISBN 978-1-932417-20-3
            Texas*Oklahoma   Hardcover 8½x11) $21.95^

^ **Save $3.00** Softcover, spiral-bound editions are also available. Recommended for light-duty, personal use only. Subtract $3.00 from standard hardcover price and ✓ here: ❑

Please add $4.00 for shipping the first volume, and $2.00 for each additional volume.

Please include your check/money order, and complete the shipping information in the indicated space below.

Total amount enclosed $_____

Name_____

Address_____

City_____ State_____ Zip_____

Please mail your completed order to:

Discovery Publishing   P.O. Box 50545   Billings, MT 59105   (Phone 1-406-861-6564)

Thank You Very Much For Your Order!

Prices, shipping charges, and specifications are subject to change.

(A photocopy or other reproduction may be substituted for this original form.)